The Treasures of My Heart

The Treasures of My Heart

Bambi Lynn

To the people—my people—who've touched my life in countless ways: I dedicate this book to you. You became my family, helped me raise my children, nursed me back to health, and gave me hope in the most devastating times of my life. You made sure I had Christmas presents, and you never forgot my birthday. You made sure I was celebrated as a mother. Some of you were just a chapter in my story and some of you are intertwined throughout it all. You've seen me fall, and you've watched me rise back up. You knew when my freezer was empty, you knew when I didn't have gas in my car, and when my children needed something that I couldn't afford, you did everything in your power to help. When my house was falling apart around me because I didn't have the money for repairs, it was all of you who stepped up to the plate without hesitation. When I was sick, you put up with my shenanigans when I'd stay in bed for an extra day or two just for the attention. You're the ones I've laughed with until I couldn't breathe and my belly hurt, and you're the ones who cried with me when I was down.

You've been the true definition of friends that 'stick closer than a brother.' Without all of you, I don't know where I'd be today. Accept this dedication as a small gesture of thanks, because words will never be able to express my gratitude! I am who I am because each and every one of you were willing to give pieces of yourselves, and in doing so, you made me whole. Thank you for never giving up on me, and most of all, for never allowing me to walk alone.

"Be careful who you call your friends. I'd rather have four quarters than 100 pennies when it comes to friendships."
~ Al Capone

Foreword

As a little girl, Bambi often felt alone and forgotten, but little did she know that her Heavenly Father was there every step of the way and that as an adult, she'd be looking back on her childhood and realize that what she'd always craved-deep, unconditional love-had been there the whole time. She only had to look for it.

In *The Treasures of My Heart*, Bambi takes a trip down memory lane, revisiting the vision God had given her, and sharing the stories behind each treasure she'd seen peeking out of the pockets of her heart. Some are lighthearted and carefree, while others may bring tears to your eyes, but from the intricate threads of her memory, Bambi takes the good and bad alike and somehow weaves it into a beautiful tapestry-a masterpiece-that emanates the goodness of God.

Throughout the pages ahead, Bambi's passion for every individual to look at their life from a new perspective shines through. The hope she narrates is the same hope that *you* have. Bambi's desire is for everyone to gain a new outlook on life, and instead of just seeing what *is,* look for the potential. Imagine. Dream. *Don't be afraid to live outside the box.* It is there, after all, that you'll realize the most cherished treasures you possess are the ones that have been in your heart all along.

Preface

In my first book, *The Journey of Josephine*, I told the story of my life. It was a raw and painfully deep account of my childhood and life until now, but it was focused on that and that alone. I made sure to stay on track and avoid going down any kind of rabbit hole. I told the story of my journey from brokenness to wholeness, trauma to triumph, unforgiveness to forgiveness, and the valleys and mountains I encountered along the way, but I didn't talk about what got me there. This book is the story of the gifts I received from my heavenly Father that have shaped me and brought me to where I am today. I've had joy and indescribable beauty throughout the journey of my life, and I embrace the words of Joseph in Genesis 20:50 where he explains the meaning and beauty he'd found in his own tragedies. *"You intended to harm me, but God intended it for good to accomplish what is now being done, the saving of many lives."* Genesis 50:20, NIV.

Prologue

Treasures are meant to be cherished. Most of the time, treasures are hidden gems that have to be searched for. They're not easily exposed. They are precious-something that isn't shared with everyone. They're often hidden; put away with the hope that they'll be found someday, giving the one to find them a chance to experience the story of why they were hidden in the first place.

Years ago, I went to a counselor; one that was different from all the rest. My whole life, therapy was just me sitting on someone's couch, telling my story as they wrote down notes. Even now, I'm not even sure if they were even listening, or were just keeping track of the clock, waiting to end the session. As a young girl, I hated therapy. My siblings and I were told it was a safe place, only to have our mom called in to discuss everything we'd told the counselor. We were yelled at all the way home for saying things we "shouldn't have said" or exaggerating the things we spoke up about.

Counseling wasn't safe for me as a child and defeated the purpose of anything changing in my house. Once I was married, counseling became something I did because I needed to be fixed. For most of my life I had been told repeatedly that I was the cause of most problems. I knew some of that was true, but what I wanted most was simply to heal from the pain that was eating me up inside. I wanted to feel normal, and I was willing to do anything to have that peace that passes all understanding, but digging up the hurt and pain of the past wasn't giving me the results I so desperately wanted. I read all the books, did the journaling, completed the homework, and with fingers crossed, clung to the belief that it would get worse before it got better. I couldn't wait much longer for the miracle of peace and healing. Unwilling to give up, I found myself attending pastoral counseling after my ex-husband had multiple affairs that resulted in him running out on me and my young children while I was pregnant.

If you just let him lead, he won't look elsewhere, and he'll stay faithful.

He isn't the problem: you need to be a better wife.

You need to change.

You need to do this.

Stop doing that.

The blame was never on him. After all, I was the broken one. I was the one with the baggage. I'd sought out church leaders for counseling and guidance, only to be given a list of things to do that would make it all better. *Just follow the list and you'll see results.*

Desperate for change, I lost myself piece by piece and was thrown back into the pit of despair because I was still broken. I poured my heart out onto the pages of my journal to ease the pain, just to have my ex-husband use what I wrote against me in arguments and eventually burn my journals, tossing the charred pages into a dumpster. Counseling wasn't working; it wasn't delivering me, and I wasn't finding peace. It led me to the do's and don'ts, but not to the peace that I needed.

As a desperate last try, I started seeing another counselor. It was a breath of fresh air. They wanted to get to the heart of things, wanted me to identify the lies I was believing, and to find peace through the peace of the truth. This counselor helped me get to the root of my past, and step-by-step helped me to see the truth revealed in a way that led me to healing; to *freedom.* It was no longer about making sure I prayed three times a day and wrote in my journal for at least an hour a day. It wasn't about "just finding the good in the day." That wasn't even an option; I no longer knew who I was anymore. I wasn't even capable of shaping my life around a list.

These sessions started with silence followed by a prayer asking God to bring me to a part of my life that had brought pain. I would wait for God to show me a scene from my life, and ask, "Where were you?" To my surprise, He was always there. I just needed to find Him. I remember once asking that question, and I was brought to the room where my mom was holding me as a newborn. Where was Jesus then? I had been told so many stories about my birth and never really found out the truth. My mom told me my dad didn't want me because I was a girl, and I was told by my dad that he was told to leave because I wasn't even his. I was told I was named Bambi because I had such big eyes. After that, it turned into my name being given to me because Bambi was a name people would remember since my mom knew my life wasn't going to be easy. My dad told me he felt such hate the moment he walked into the room, and my mom told me he was extremely drunk. If I was born into such hatred, why wasn't Jesus there to soften it? As I looked around the room, I saw Him. He stood at the foot of the bed, gentle and reassuring like the loving Father He is. He wasn't speaking, but I could feel him telling me He'd formed me in my mother's womb, that He knew me, and that He had a purpose for me. Each time I went to a session, we would do the same thing. We identified the lies that I was believing, and then, one by one, we uncovered the truth behind each lie. I went back each week and began working through the lies in my life. These sessions were painful, and the hurt ran deep, but I needed to get to the truth.

I vividly remember a session working through a specific incident that happened when I was just a little girl. We were renting a big white farmhouse with a front porch, a garden, and a herd of pigs. I don't think we were responsible for the animals or the garden, but they were there since we just rented the house on the property.

My brother, who was allergic to everything, had run into the garden and eaten something. I ran to him and told him to spit it out because he was going to die if he swallowed it. I was only five years old. Later that evening, we were in bed and my brother started screaming that he was going to die. When asked why he thought that, he said, "Bambi said I was."
I was called down the stairs. My mom was sitting in a chair, legs crossed and her hands deftly knitting something.

My dad was on the couch. As I stood in front of my dad, he took off his belt, and to this day I can hear the belt being pulled through his belt loops. The thought of it still makes me cringe. My mom sat in the chair, never even looking up. As the belt bit into my back, my dad screamed at me to never talk to his son that way. I don't remember how long that beating lasted, but I remember feeling his hatred towards me even years later. I felt vulnerable and unsafe.

I was angry with God for putting me into a family in which I had no worth. This would turn out to be a difficult session to find God in. I had carried that hate toward Him for so long. I couldn't stop the tears from falling, and I couldn't even fight the hate I held in my heart. I screamed, "Where are you? Where were you? Why didn't you come?" And I waited for His response. I was so firmly convinced he wasn't there, but that belief started to crumble when I saw Him walking into the room and placing His hand on my dad's shoulder, pushing him to stop. Jesus was crying; I saw His tears. I once again saw His compassion. I felt his love. I experienced His love coming to my rescue. I felt true peace.

Even though my dad still beat me and spewed such hatred toward me, Jesus showed me the opposite. He didn't stop the beating from happening, but He did come in and end it.

I could now open my eyes and look at my counselor and say, "He really was there." The enemy wants us to believe that we've been forsaken, but we need to understand we have not been: Jesus really does love us, and He will prove it over and over again.

That was a time that I needed to understand more than ever. I needed God to show me He had shown up. I know to some people this kind of counseling sounds so far-fetched, but it comes from Jeremiah 6:16-17. *Ask for the ancient paths, ask where the good way is, and walk in it, and you will find rest for your soul.*

I had to find out the truth of my past and see Jesus in it for me to grow my faith in Him. I had to put Jesus to the test and find Him in every part of my life. I had to find Him in the times when I couldn't see through the pain, and believe He never left me. Each dark moment in my life had me believing that He never cared, and when I went on this journey and realized just how much He did care, my faith multiplied. Searching out His truth and His ways led me to an intensely deeper faith in him.

I still had areas of life where I had to look for Him and wait for Him to show me His presence. This wasn't ever easy, and it was never a quick fix in my belief system, but it was my journey of discovering Him and His true love for me.

When I found myself in a second abusive marriage, I had to rely heavily on knowing who I was and not accepting the lies that were told to me daily. When my three daughters left to move in with their dad because of the abuse they were witnessing, my life went dark. I fell into a pit of despair, and I didn't know if I would ever breathe again. *How do you survive when your whole world walks away?*

I went to my counselor and cried on her lap, soaking us both with my tears.

"Go to God, Bambi," she told me. "Give Him a chance to show you His vision for your girls."

I held so much anger in my heart, knowing His vision wasn't *my* vision. I felt like a failure: an empty shell broken into little pieces that would never again be whole.

Defeated and hurting, I finally found the courage to seek out God's truth. Once my heart was open to Him once more, God showed me three cocoons that were opening. As the cocoons opened, I saw three of the most beautiful butterflies I've ever seen fly away.

For the first time, I was seeing the whole experience through the eyes of my daughters. Their leaving was freedom for them for them to grow. The beauty of the butterflies' wings was a symbol that this was good for them.

My pain was still present, and I knew it was going to stay. Despite my own hurt, I knew my girls needed to blossom and the toxic environment they'd been living in was hindering that.

I was still reeling from the shock of it all, and the severe depression it caused pushed my body into premature menopause. Through all of it, the vision God had given to me gave me hope for my daughters: reassurance that they were going to be okay.

Where was Jesus in all of this? He was right there, giving my daughters a way of escape and showing me that mine was coming.

One of the last sessions I had with my counselor is the foundation of this book: the vision that God showed me, helping me see the rest of my story through His eyes.

Once again, I found myself praying for God to show me something to show me that He had always been there in the midst of all the pain throughout my life. I wanted to know what kept me alive throughout this life that seemed to try to suffocate me whichever way turned.

As I sat with my eyes closed and my heart ready, I saw a human heart. Not a paper heart that you'd cut out as a child, but the heart that was beating within me.

I was kind of awestruck by it, wondering what it meant. Then, I noticed little pockets throughout the heart, each one with a little gift tucked inside it.

I saw objects, experiences—I saw *blessings.* I saw things I hold dear to my heart that were from the parts of my life where I had been in the deepest pain. God *had* been holding my heart all along.

From the beginning of time, He held my heart, and had been placing little treasures in it: gifts from His father-heart that He revealed to me one-by-one at the precise moments of my life when I needed them most.

To some it may look like a survival kit, but to me it was a treasure box: *the treasures of my heart.*

Josephine Priscilla

One of the first treasures I saw peeking out of my heart was a handmade rag doll I was given as a Christmas gift when I was a child. I named her Josephine Priscilla after a little girl in a movie I'd seen: *Orphan Train*. Josephine was with me throughout my life, even into adulthood. She brought me comfort in the darkness. She kept my secrets, never to tell a soul. She was my security blanket as I navigated my childhood in an abusive and unstable home. She caught my tears when I told her of the abuse I endured at the hands of my grandfather, my uncle, and other dirty old men. She was there for me when I gave myself to men who didn't deserve me as I searched for love, only to come home empty and brokenhearted. Josephine journeyed with me into marriages that ultimately shattered, destroyed by infidelity and domestic violence. She watched when my life spiraled out of control and was there when I surrendered everything to Jesus. Josephine carried my sadness when I had nobody to talk to. When I had nothing to hold, she was there. Whenever life seemed to fall apart, she was always there.

Each time my children left the nest, especially my twin sons, she was there. When the house was quiet and only the walls could talk, she was there. She was there in the hotels when I began to travel for work, and I'd come home to her sitting on the back of the couch.

I don't rely on her like I did in my earlier days of turmoil, but her presence still comforts my heart when I walk into my guest bedroom and see her sitting on the headboard. Her days of carrying me along through the pain of life and the destruction of so many lives are over. She no longer needs to carry my tears or be a listening ear to the secrets of my life. Her role in my life now is simply being one of my greatest treasures. That small ragdoll that I was given so many years ago was the inspiration for my first book, *The Journey of Josephine: The Doll that Mended a Broken Heart.* I'd never dreamed I'd be an author, but in July of 2023, I was holding a published book—*my book*—and it was all because of Josephine. I documented our journey together from the very start, went through the editing process, and finally published it. My heart is still

overwhelmed by the fact that *my* story is a
published book.

When I close my eyes and remember that
vision of my heart with the little pockets of
treasures, I am thankful that God made her the
most noticeable. She will always be something
that I hold close to my heart. A jewel, a rare gift,
and a cherished treasure that God hid in my heart.

The Little Stable

The next treasure that caught my eye was a small wooden stable I had made with my dad when I was a child. My dad didn't have much interaction with me. Our relationship wasn't an emotional one; I was simply his biological offspring. I was told repeatedly just how much he disliked me. I remember his drunken slurs, telling me I wasn't even his.

For most of my early childhood, my dad was in and out of my life. He was an angry and abusive alcoholic. As a result, most of the memories I have of him are of him being drunk, and watching my mom being battered around by him. I have memories of him forcing us to sit on the couch, and then screaming at us, and telling me I didn't belong to him. He was never the kind of dad that made you feel safe. He wasn't one of those 'fun dads' that took you places and made you feel special.

I had to go to work with him once for some reason, and I wore a white dress and white sandals. He was upset at my choice of attire but didn't make me change. He was picking up used cooking oil from different restaurants, and as I watched him, he slipped and fell right into the bucket of oil. I still find it funny that he was upset I wore white but was the one who got all greasy.

I remember riding between my mom's legs on the floor of his truck while my brother and sister rode behind the seat in the sleeper cab, and at night, sleeping in the cars he was delivering. At one of the stops, there were huge logs lying around by the parking lot, and my siblings and I ate our lunch there, perched up on the logs like birds.

I took the brunt of his rude words and harsh treatment. A painful example of this, ironic as it may be, happened in church. He'd been asked to sing "The Old Rugged Cross," and he'd asked my brother and sister if they wanted to come up to sing with him. I stood up, excited to sing with them, but received a cruel look instead of the smile my siblings had gotten.

"I didn't ask you, Bambi." I remember the sting of that short sentence like it was yesterday.

I remember feeling crushed and ashamed that I embarrassed myself by getting up to walk on stage to sing with him.

I felt so *empty.* I craved my father's love and never got it. Not only that, but I watched my siblings receive the love I so desperately wanted, and it broke me down, piece by piece.

He was like that my whole life, but that brings me back to the stable I saw peeking out of my heart. God had placed this barn in one of those pockets, knowing it would be a treasure that helps me even today to feel a sense of connection with my dad.

My mom had wanted a stable made for her Nativity set. My dad offered to make it, and looked over at me, much to my surprise.

"Bambi, come outside with me." *He wanted me.*

I was the only kid out there with him, as my siblings stood inside behind the glass patio door, watching us.

We cut the planks, breathing in the sweet scent of fresh cut wood. My little girl-heart swelled with emotion as I helped him put the pieces together. I still get those silly feelings in my heart whenever I think of those few moments with him.

My relationship with my dad had always been difficult. However, many years later my dad came back into my life, and we worked on reconciling our relationship. It was slow and painful. My parents had split up when I was ten, and he wasn't really around after that. How do you reconcile a relationship based on bad memories?

He was a hard man who'd lived a hard life. I don't think he even knew how to love. His generation didn't talk about their feelings or acknowledge past traumas. I knew my dad had endured a rough and abusive childhood with an alcoholic father. His brothers and he, himself, had destroyed relationships because of the bottle, just like their father before them.

Dad had gone to rehab a few times, but it never lasted. I was told that he got sober after his split with my mom, but even sober, he was an angry and bitter man who felt he'd never gotten a break in life.

My dad came to my house after that, attempting to build relationships with my children and telling me stories of what he felt went on in the marriage with my mom.

There are always two sides to every story, told through the hurt of your own heart. Viewing my dad from that perspective helped me understand his actions a little more, but there was still a nagging question that I was too scared to ask; scared that the answer might hurt more than not knowing.

One day, my dad called me and he brought up how hard things were for him and how he loved us kids, and how my mom was, well, my *mom*. Exhausted from the constant wondering, I blurted out my question:

"Why didn't you love me?" I cried. "Why did you hate me so much? Why did you make sure I knew how much you *didn't* love me?" I waited for the answer to my question, taking deep breaths to prepare my heart and my body for the answer that was coming.

"Bambi, I was always told you weren't mine,"
he said. The pain in his voice was so heavy I
could physically feel it.

Now it was out there-the truth that he'd
believed. It was the reason he had always been
consumed with hate for me. It was why he so
coldly walked away from me in the room
where I was born. The things he was told that
day? They were the things responsible for all
his anger towards me.

That was the first time I'd heard my dad cry.
I heard the regret in his voice, the pain in his
heart, and the remorse gnawing away at his
very soul, and the wishing he could change the
way he'd treated me for all of my childhood. I
heard his broken betrayal and the suffering he
endured when he was constantly reminded that
I would never be his. My dad told me how
sorry he was on that day, apologizing over and
over. He told me he loved me, that I was just a
child, and how he should've never said or did
all those terrible things he said to me when I
was just a little girl. I forgave my dad that day.
Even now, I haven't searched out the answers
to all of that. I have spoken to different people
in my family on both sides, but I learned to let
it go.

Looking back at it all brings me back to that
stable. I understood why God put that as one of
my treasures. I understand now a bit of what
God was thinking when He put it there: a little
piece of happiness with my dad.

When I think of all my past sorrow, I also
think of that moment outside with him, making

a stable for baby Jesus. I was given a moment that doesn't erase the sadness but rather softens it. Before my dad passed, I wrote a letter to him reminiscing on some of my memories with him, pouring out my love to the man that spent half my life not even knowing I was his. It read,

"Dear Dad,
I want to first tell you that I forgive you, and I have no ill will towards you. So many things run through my mind, things that happened throughout my life, and things that I have let go. I want you to know that I know that you tried your best. We lived in a different kind of world, and sometimes we had so much pain in our lives that we didn't know how to cope with it and your way of coping was making the decisions that you did. Life is different now and as you get older you see things in a different way. You don't hold grudges towards people but rather put yourself in their shoes. You asked me what I would do with the same kind of decisions and scenarios that you had to live through. The memories that I have, even though they are few, are memories that I still cherish. I know that April showed you the manger that you made, and she said that you didn't remember who made it with you but you do remember making it. Well, it was me that you made it with. It's the only thing that we did together without anyone else. Todd and Laurie were standing at the glass doors watching while you and I were outside putting it together. I put that manger scene up every Christmas and reminisce on that day. I was telling April today of the time that I had to go to work with you when you were picking up cooking oil from restaurants, and I was all dressed up because that just was the kind of little girl that I was and you fell into a

grease bucket and you were the one that got dirty that day and not me. It makes me laugh! I remember when we went to church at that Southern Baptist church in Virginia and you would sing The Old Rugged Cross. You never wanted me to sing it with you, but every time I hear that song I hear you singing it and it makes me smile. I thought it was kind of ironic that the day that I was in labor with Amber, you showed up to pick up Kenny at my mom's house. I was going to give birth that day to your first grandchild and you just happened to be there. Years later when I lived in Silver Springs we started to have some kind of relationship again and you would buy big stuffed animals and candy for my girls. When I moved to Buffalo you came out to visit us. One day you came into my house and told me that you wanted bacon and eggs. And a cup of coffee. You didn't say hi to me, you didn't even say thank you, but just demanded the bacon and eggs and coffee. I was so mad that day, but it makes me laugh now because that's just the kind of person that you were. I called you once and I asked you some really hard questions and told you I wanted the answers and that I didn't want you to lie to me. You poured out your heart to me, and I knew that wasn't easy for you, but it gave me closure. I want to thank you for being so honest even though it was hard. I want to thank you for not running away from the questions I asked and giving me the answers that I needed, and for really living up to your responsibility towards me and how you treated me as a little girl. I want you to know that meant a lot to me. You haven't had it easy and that I understand. I remember as a little girl going to Grandma and Grandpa's house and realizing what you went through. Those were some really tough times. I just wanted you to know that as the last days of your life are approaching, we are all okay.

You know that I have 12 living grandchildren and one of my grandsons, Isaac, passed away nine hours after he was born, but boy do I love being a Nona. I know that you didn't always get a chance to be part of our lives and to be part of my children's lives but I know you wanted to. After 25 years of living in Buffalo, I moved to Georgia. It is so funny to me because I thought that I would live in that house forever, but three out of my six children live in the South so during the pandemic I sold everything and I moved here. I'm doing okay! I am living a good life. I travel a lot, and I may not travel in a semi and see the country in a big truck, but I have been to 42 of the 50 states. Every time I see a semi-truck that carries cars I think about the times when I was a little girl and I had to sit between mom's legs when we were driving, and how at night time we slept inside of the cars that you were delivering. I remember stopping at this one place that had logs around the parking lot and we all sat and ate our lunch on them. The things that I remember...

I am taking my grandchildren all across the country and have had some very special times with them building incredible memories. I am giving my grandchildren a good life and for some reason I wanted you to know that. Dad, I want you to know that I am okay, and that I'm going to be okay. I want you to know that I love you! Once again, I forgive you. When you close your eyes for the last time, know that you go in peace and I have nothing against you! I hope God allows you to sing The Old Rugged Cross as you meet Him.
Love, Bambi."

When my half-sister read the letter to him, he remembered. He remembered, and that is all I needed: that little treasure that God made sure was mine and mine alone.

Even though my dad is gone now, that moment is forever tucked away in my heart. When I think of the past and the pain with my dad, I have that moment he gave to me, and it brings me peace. This treasure that was hidden in my heart continues to bless me every Christmas, and when I bring it out and display that little stable with my porcelain nativity figurines, it serves as a tangible reminder that even though my dad may not have given me much, he gave me this precious memory that I will forever cherish in my heart— little treasure, hidden away just for me.

The Banana Split

My next treasure I saw was a banana split. It made me chuckle when I saw it, because it was from my uncle Donald and his then-girlfriend, Francis, whom he married later on.

We had moved to Virginia when I was eight because my dad said he had changed and wasn't drinking anymore, and my mom agreed to give him another chance.

My uncle came over to visit a lot, and always brought Francis. Francis was the fluffiest person I'd ever seen, with a jolly personality to match. She was bubbly, funny, and the sweetest person I'd ever met. My uncle was, understandably, completely smitten with her.

I was having a hard time in school and struggling with my schoolwork. Trying to fit in and make friends was a battle in itself. My siblings and I were all in school, but it was me that Uncle Donald devoted himself to, and after realizing how much I was struggling, he offered me a contest. He said if I got straight A's for one week, he and Francis would take me out for ice cream, and I could have anything I wanted.

I was thrilled, not just about the ice cream but about the fact that it was *me* Uncle Donald had chosen. I dedicated myself to my schoolwork for the entire week. The ice cream was a nice reward, but making them proud mattered to me even more. Just knowing that they believed in me made me try harder in school.

Every day, I did my absolute best in school. I couldn't bear the thought of disappointing my uncle Donald and Francis. Every day I came home with an A. I couldn't believe it. Every day, they cheered me on and told me they were proud of me, and I counted down the days until they would take me out. Friday came, and I had received all A's that week. I got into the car and they took me to the nearest ice cream shop. I chose a banana split. Our family didn't have money to go out for ice cream, let alone anything bigger than a cone. I got to pick all my toppings and the flavors of ice cream that I wanted.

We sat at the table, and I tried with everything in me to eat and finish my banana split, but all it did was make me sick. They didn't get mad at me and tell me I wasted money, but rather told me how proud they were of me for getting all A's for the week.

It was never about ice cream, but about the treasure they gave me by making me feel important in the chaotic world that I was living in.

I've always remembered that time with such fondness, and I thank God for putting that little treasure in my heart to remind me that there *were* people who care—people who saw a struggling little girl and gave her a gift by making her feel seen.

Even now, I still don't like ice cream. I thought I did for years, and I'd buy it just to have it sit in the freezer and never be touched. Eventually, I realized that what I thought was a fondness for ice cream was simply the sweet memories I have associated with it. With that memory tucked away in my heart like a tiny jewel, I don't need to have ice cream to remember it or the emotions I have tied to it.

Treasures are meant to be found, and I am so grateful that this one was hidden away where I could find it and thank God for his caring love for me.

My Cousins

One of the greatest treasures that I saw in the pockets of my heart was my cousins. My whole childhood I was raised next door to my cousins. I believe growing up with your cousins is one of the greatest joys a child can experience.

My cousins and I spent long, fun-filled days running around the baseball field, having walnut wars in the woods, and building forts together. We made hospitals in a dugout, played dodgeball in the backyard, and we had so much fun. We'd come up with 'food' made of whatever we'd scrounged up in the woods and try to feed it to the younger cousins as a sort of initiation into our club.

There was a garage next to our house that we would clean all the time and plan parties in, knowing we'd never actually throw the parties since none of us had money, but imagining and laughing at the thought of them just the same. We spent hours on our front porch, laughing, telling jokes, and living the best life ever with each other.

In my eyes, my aunt and uncle were the coolest people ever. One of my favorite things about their house was the treat drawer they had for my cousins. I remember sneaking into their house just to grab a snack from the drawer. We never had that kind of stuff at my house. I didn't understand it was stealing then, although I do now.

My aunt played a huge role in my life, and I looked at her as a mother figure. She once saved me when I was choking on a root beer barrel candy. She was also the person I went to when I got my first period. She was always there for me, and I loved her for it.

Even as a parent, I made sure to always have a snack cabinet or snack freezer for the neighborhood kids because of my aunt and uncle.

At Christmastime, my cousins would get the best gifts and always got lots of candy in their stockings. To me, my aunt and uncle were rich. It's funny how young minds look at the things around them.

My cousins were a safe haven for me as a child. We shared so much laughter together. I remember playing chicken on our front porch once, and I laughed so hard I accidentally peed on the shoulders of the person carrying me. I jumped down and ran and as I was running away, I heard the unfortunate victim of my accident say with confusion in their voice, "My shoulder is wet." To this day I have never told that person I was the one who peed on them, but I laugh every time I remember that story.

My uncle told me one time that my parents picked me up from a grocery store, right off the shelf, and when they wanted to return me the store manager told them no. He had me convinced and crying over that.

My fondest memories as a child always included my cousins. I had another friend that was my next-door neighbor and we spent hours playing badminton, riding bikes in the summer heat, and building snowmen and having snowball fights when winter came. The imagination of play I had with my cousins was by far the best part of growing up.

When my cousins moved to the country and no longer lived next door, there was a lot of sadness. Our lives were intertwined with each other. I suffered a great loss of security and true friendships. They knew our lives and how hard they were, but they were always there. I'm so thankful for them and the times we shared. We were innocent in those days, and our times together took a lot of pain away.

I look back with the fondest memories and thank God for that little piece of happiness. Treasures are meant to be cherished, and this is one I'll always hold close to my heart.

The Old Bus

The next treasure that caught my eye was an old school bus. Every Sunday when I was a child, that bus would stop by my house and pick my siblings and me up to take us to church.

The church that we attended had a bus ministry that picked up kids from the surrounding neighborhoods to bring them to and from church. I wasn't surprised to see that bus tucked away in my heart. I can't even explain the excitement I felt every Sunday getting up to go to church. I was one of few that didn't see it as drudgery. Some of my fondest memories were on that bus. We'd sing Sunday school songs all the way there and all the way back: songs that have been ingrained in my mind, and that I still sing to my own grandchildren every chance I get.

I remember the bus driver with his black top hat perched on his head. He'd tell us stories of Jesus and the love that He had.

I never felt like part of the church family as a child. The 'church kids' looked down on us bus kids, but that never mattered to me. I knew that just being there made me happy.
I was small enough then that I'd have to be carried up the bus stairs. My mom didn't come to church with us just like most parents. To a lot of them, it was their child-free time. However, that didn't matter to me either.

I felt so safe at church. Some of the other bus kids would make fun of me because I was so enthusiastic and would get carried away as we'd sing and clap our hands, but I didn't care.
When we'd get dropped off at the door for Sunday school and then junior church, I was the first one off the bus, ready to go to class and listen to the Bible stories.

Once, I had to go to the bathroom and when I left my class to go, a little boy came out of nowhere, running down the stairs and right into me, knocking me down. I was rushed to the hospital and was told when I was older that they were surprised that I never lost my vision or even my eye because I'd been hit so hard that my eye was swollen and hanging down.

The bus driver and his assistant sometimes came to my home to check on me and make sure I was okay, and it always made me feel so important and special.

The very first time I was ever taken to a restaurant was because of a Sunday school contest that I'd won. My teacher took me to the Country Kitchen in Mt. Morris, and I ordered chicken and mashed potatoes. She made me feel so special. Funny enough, years later I would end up marrying her grandson, although I didn't know him at the time. His Grandma was one of my favorite teachers.

When I'd get home from Sunday school every week, I'd practice my Bible verses until I could recite them perfectly. If we memorized them, we'd get stickers as a prize, and that's also how I got to go to a restaurant for the first time: memorizing verses.

Another Sunday School teacher would take us to Burger king if we behaved in his class. He'd get permission from our parents, take us to Burger King, and let us order anything we wanted. I think a lot of kids took advantage of his kindness, but he didn't seem to notice. I think he knew that regardless of how some of the kids behaved, they'd always remember him.

Whenever I'd get on the church bus, I felt like I was home. I loved going to church so much. Ignoring the other kids sitting in the back of church, coloring on the pews, being loud and being rude, I was sitting up front soaking up the sermons and stories about Jesus.

I was given the opportunity to help teach during junior church and was even able to lead a little girl to Jesus. I wasn't yet a Christian because in my mind, Jesus wouldn't come into the heart of a little girl that came on the church bus, but I would tell the other little children all about Jesus. I just wanted them to be loved.

Some of the rides to and from church were long depending on the kids and sometimes families that needed to be dropped off before us, but I didn't care. All I did care about was being able to sing to Jesus and feeling loved.

Looking back, that church bus helped me throughout my younger years even more than I realized at the time. I know that the seeds were planted in my heart for me to one day surrender to Jesus. All those songs I memorized and loved singing so much still encourage me even as an adult. In the moments of my life where I was in the dark, and when I was so discouraged, I couldn't find the words to pray, God gave me a song. I can still feel the hope that came over me in those moments.

That church bus stuck out in my heart because God was reminding me that he has never left me nor forsaken me. He's had a plan for me since before I was even a thought.

The bus was a lifeline to me in the darkest of times. To others, the honk of the horn in front of their homes early on a Sunday morning may have brought discouragement, but to me it was a ray of sunshine: another chance to hear about Jesus. What a treasure to have hidden in my heart; one to cherish for a lifetime.

The Little Bible

As I began to understand the purpose of each treasure as they were revealed to me, I got more excited with each one. I realized that they were my safe place on my journey. They brought me comfort—a reprieve—from the brokenness that I was carrying.

The next treasure I noticed was my very first Bible. The sight of it brought overwhelming joy to my heart. I'd learned so much with that precious Bible.

This Bible had been given to me by the Conklin's, a family in the church I went to as a child. Although I've already told the story of my church bus experience, this family would take me to church Sunday night and Wednesday. They'd pick me up no matter the weather— rain, sleet, or snow. They were dedicated to making sure I got to church. They saw the softness of my child-heart; my yearning to have more of Jesus.

The Conklin's had two children at the time, and I was an added passenger in their little car every time the church doors were open and I couldn't get there on the bus. They took me under their wing and showed me Jesus in a way I'd never seen before. His love emanated from them, almost like *they* were Jesus with human skin on. They were gentle with me, and so understanding and kind. I'm sure their two children didn't particularly enjoy being squished in the backseat of their car just for the sake of a young, loudmouthed girl who never stopped talking, but I never heard them complain. I don't know how far they had to drive out of their way for me, or even how or why they'd volunteered to take charge of transportation for a young girl who was hungry to learn about this gentle man named Jesus. They didn't know about my home life or the abuse and dysfunction I endured every day. I never spoke about it. Despite not knowing any of my back story, the Conklin's brought healing and hope to my broken self; they made me feel as if I belonged, and they'd given me the greatest gift in that small Bible. Every service, I'd listen intently and write and underline in my Bible. I'd jot down quotes in it, underline special passages, and learn memory verses. I felt so *loved* with this special gift. I had that Bible for years and years, and when its tattered pages began to fall apart, I put it away for safekeeping so I could always remember how special it was to me.

I felt blessed to have the Conklin's in my life, and their willingness to do whatever they could to help me seek Jesus touched my heart. I wanted to be at church every time the doors were open, and they turned that desire into a reality.

One Sunday night, my mom told me I wasn't going to be able to go to church. I began to cry, but my tears only angered her. She jumped on top of me, biting me and pulling my hair. She She told me I only wanted to go to church because of the boys that were there. Some of the boys in the youth group *were* cute, but that was far from what fed my desire to be there. I wanted to go because it felt peaceful; I felt at home.

I was treated differently on Wednesday and Sunday nights. I wasn't a church bus kid, but someone who actually had a place there and that made me feel special. My mom couldn't understand that, but I knew it in my heart.

At age fourteen I left the church. We'd had a youth meeting, and at the meeting we were told that a girl had gotten pregnant, and since she'd made an adult decision, we weren't allowed to talk to her or hang out with her.

I was so devastated that I never went back. I didn't understand why or how a church that preached love and forgiveness could treat someone like that.

I didn't see the Conklin's for a while after that, but when we did rekindle a relationship, it was an actual friendship and not just them caring for a young girl that needed help.

The Conklin's were the ones that introduced me to homeschooling. They'd pulled their son and daughter out of the Christian school and began teaching them at home.

Homeschooling was an odd concept at the time, but it was one that stuck with me. Their son learned to play the piano and their daughter began playing the violin. I'd never heard children play the way they did. I could've listened for hours and hours. It was so beautiful it took my breath away. Pam and I became good friends, and since I'd had children by that point, I looked up to her for guidance. Although I didn't always agree with her, she was the woman Titus 2 speaks about: the older woman teaching the younger, and we confided in each other on what God was doing in our lives. She even asked me to watch her children one year while she went to a church Christmas party.

One Christmas Eve, the Conklin's invited my girls and me to a Christmas Eve get-together. It was the worst snowstorm I'd ever driven in, but the evening was the sweetest and purest gathering I'd ever experienced. To this day I'm still not sure how I made it home, but it was worth it.

My friendship with the Conklin's, as well as the Bible they'd given me, were precious and I held both close to my heart. I had that Bible up until my ex-husband took a box of precious things of mine and my daughters', burned it, and threw the remains in a dumpster. The pain of that loss was difficult to grieve and to let go, because that Bible held so many memories for me. However, my friendship with the Conklin's is still a sweet and dear part of me, and they're a solid pillar in my life.

God brought them to help hold me together in some very dark times. His timing is always perfect, giving us the little treasures we need exactly when we need them. Some of them are temporary, but many of them last a lifetime.

My Grandma

A treasure doesn't lose its value just because it's no longer in your possession. There is something special about having something of value in your life that keeps giving you the feeling of belonging even after it's gone.
I saw my grandma peeking out of one of my heart's pockets. Even though she's been gone for many years, the warmth of her presence still brings peace to me as I look back fondly on my memories of her.

My grandma was a safe place for me. My first book and autobiography, "The Journey of Josephine," mentions the story of my grandfather fondling me as a little girl and the sexual abuse I experienced at his hands. Knowing that, it would only make sense that I'd be afraid to stay at my grandma's house, but in my mind, I was able to separate the trauma from the good because of the love that I had for my grandma.

I never exposed my grandfather until weeks after my grandma had passed away. I loved her far too much to share something that I knew would destroy her.

My grandma made me feel special whenever I was around her. We'd moved in and out of my grandma's house every time my parents' marriage spiraled and whenever my dad's drinking was bad.

When we weren't living with my grandparents, we were close by, either in a close apartment building or across the street.

I walked by grandma's house every day for school. It was the white house on the corner block, and one of the prettiest houses on the street. Whenever I'd walk in the door, my nose was greeted by the scent of freshly baked cookies and dove soap. My grandma's house was where I learned about being hospitable to guests and creating an atmosphere of peace.

She taught me to clean, and to clean well, by always leaving little things in the corners or hidden in random places so that she could tell if I vacuumed and dusted or not.

When my family got together during the holidays, all my cousins and I would sit on grandma's stairs and dream of getting married near the fireplace and walking down her elegant staircase. Her house was the one place where we could dream the biggest dreams and it still felt as if they'd come true.

The house was magical during the holidays. We weren't allowed to be there the day after Thanksgiving, because she'd be preparing a winter wonderland and hiding the elf that we'd scramble to find as soon as we got home from school, because whoever found the elf got a piece of candy.

There was no yelling or name calling at grandma's house, and I never felt on edge like I did at home. I didn't have to tiptoe around, walking on eggshells for fear of setting someone off. There was an almost tangible sense of calmness and safety. It was always neat and orderly—a vast difference from mine, which was cluttered, chaotic, and loud.

Whenever I'd spend the night there, I got to take showers and use Dove soap, the scent of which still brings a sense of calmness to me even today.

Grandma was fashionable and always seemed 'cool' even though she was older. I remember her letting me wear her brown jumpsuit to a youth group function and feeling like I was cool.

Although grandma didn't talk much, she listened intently. I'd cry, asking her over and over again if I could just live with her. We had a bond that I didn't have with anyone else, and I just wanted to be safe with her and her love.

Eventually, grandma sold that white house on the corner and moved away. I didn't see her much after that, because I had gotten married, and all the pain and abuse that I had endured from my grandfather and other dirty men in my life was taking its toll on me. It brought a distance between my grandma and me, not because I didn't love her, but because I didn't want to hurt her with the truth about my grandfather.

Occasionally we'd talk on the phone and laugh about old times, reminiscing on years gone by. She'd tell me how I would carry the torch of her hospitality towards people and promised me her red dishes to serve my future guests.

The last time I talked to her, she was in the hospital, and she made my grandfather promise that he would give me those dishes. I never did receive the dishes. Grandma passed away peacefully on a quiet Christmas morning. A few weeks later, I broke my silence and told the family what I had experienced at the hands of my grandfather. Other family members spoke up and the stories of what they'd gone through confirmed the horror of what my grandfather was capable of. My grandfather, upon being exposed, took off and in the process, he got rid of all of my grandma's possessions. None of us received a single thing from her.

He robbed my grandma of many things in her last few years of life, but the love grandma gave to me was something he could never take away.

Her love for me is a treasure, hidden in a pocket of my heart, and every once in a while, it

peeks out and reminds me that treasures last a
lifetime when they are as rare as my grandma.

The Red and White Pom Poms

When I saw little red and white pom poms sticking out of one of the pockets, a warm feeling flooded my heart.

I'd been a cheerleader for a couple of years in middle school. I'd worked extremely hard to get noticed, trying to find a way to get in with the in-group of girls. I wasn't anything special or even someone that they wanted to hang out with, but when I made the squad, I was ecstatic.

Middle school had been difficult for me to say the least. I was bullied constantly resulting in me always looking over my shoulder, anticipating the next cruel prank. I found myself hiding in the bushes, waiting for the other kids to get on their buses just to avoid the heartless name-calling in the halls. I sported a black eye for a few days after being punched in the face by a classmate and that same classmate shoved me down a flight of stairs and got us both suspended, all because she thought I liked her boyfriend. When I got home, my mom refused to listen to what happened, even though it wasn't my fault, and then promptly grounded me. Despite it all, however, I was overjoyed when I made the cheerleading team.

I made my first best friend, Beth, during one cheerleading season. She took me under her wing and treated me with sincere kindness. In fact, I still reread her entry in my yearbook occasionally. It reads,

"Bambi, I want you to know I'll always be here for you, and I hope you'll be there for me. I hope we remain best friends forever, and never lose your smile! We've shared so much together, and we tell each other everything. I hope all your dreams and wishes come true, and don't worry about what other people say or think. Keep that smile...and you'll get whatever you want! Love, your sis Beth."

I didn't have nice things like the rest of the girls on the cheerleading team, I had to find rides to the games that weren't held at my school, and I knew some of the girls were bothered to have me around because of those things. My new best friend, however, didn't care in the least. She even invited me to her sleepover birthday party. I had to borrow a sleeping bag because I didn't own one. All the girls wanted to watch a scary movie, and so we watched "Friday the 13th." I was so scared that I peed in the sleeping bag and didn't get out of it until morning, because I didn't want any of the other girls to make fun of me and tell the whole school. When I did get up, I hid the sleeping bag in the closet and never told a soul.

Being part of the cheerleading squad not only taught me a lot, but it gave me a little bit of **self-confidence and helped me believe in myself.**

When I hurt my arm falling off my bike, I still cheered because I didn't want anyone to think I couldn't do it and make fun of me. I was in my head a lot and made silly mistakes during competitions, because I was so scared of being made fun of.

Even with all that, there was something about walking into school on Fridays with my cheerleading outfit on that still makes me smile today. The actual cheerleading didn't mean as much to me, but the sense of belonging it gave me was something I cherished. It didn't matter if most of the girls ignored or didn't like me; I still was part of something.

My coaches did their best to make me feel special. They knew I didn't have what everyone else did, but I earned my spot through hard work, whether they would've preferred someone else or not.

And so, for a time, I *belonged.* I don't have words to express the trauma and bullying I endured throughout all my school years, but for those few seasons, I was a part of something; I had a place. The girls didn't have to like me, but the feeling of belonging was something I hadn't felt by many people.

God planted that gift in my life during a time where I was learning and discovering myself. That little girl I was getting to know hid a lot of pain in those years, but God in his everlasting love gave her a moment in a little red and white cheerleading outfit and black and white saddle shoes, holding her pom poms: the moment of belonging.

That time was a cherished treasure for me, and although it only lasted two football seasons, it still impacts my life even to this day.

The Book

The truth of each hidden pocket was meant to show me that I was never left alone, and so every time I saw another treasure, I began to understand *what* each thing had given to me, as well as the *why* behind it.

I saw the pages of a book and knew in an instant which book it was.

In seventh grade, I had a teacher that was far from nice and not at all personable. She was very blunt, set in her ways, and her clothing style was quite out of date.

One day, she handed out books to all her students. I'd never really read anything like it before. I'd read short little books, but nothing like the chapter book I held in my hands. Who read chapter books in seventh grade anyhow?

We were told this would be our assignment for the quarter. We'd be doing projects and different assignments all based on this book.

I turned the book over. "Where the Red Fern Grows," it read. I had no idea that this book would not just change the way I felt about reading but would change my life. I went home that day, started reading, and was carried away on a journey in the pages of the book.

The book was about a young boy that lived in a dilapidated old house that was more of a shack than anything else. His parents, who were sharecroppers, worked long, hard days trying to make ends meet. The boy wanted a coon dog for hunting, and his parents just didn't have the money. He found odd jobs and worked as hard as he could to make enough money to buy himself two coon dogs that he'd seen advertised in the newspaper. Finally, one day he walked into the corner store and ordered his coon dogs, as proud as could be. He waited and waited, and every day he went to the store to see if they had been delivered. When the day came to pick up his dogs, nothing could take away from his joy. He picked up *his* dogs, took them home, and named them Little Ann and Big Dan.

The story goes on about the life of the dogs and the mischief they got into. It was the first time I'd ever experienced the feeling of a story truly captivating my emotions. I could feel the excitement in the book. Who knew that a book could take you on such an adventure? I had no idea how a story could transport you into the pages of it, making you feel as if you were right there. I'd never realized that a book could make you emotional; they could make you cry. That book created the foundation of my love for reading. To this day, my love of books is because of the very first one I was forced to read in middle school. Reading takes you places that you may never physically visit. It can carry you right to the middle of a field of flowers and make it feel so real that you can smell the sweet fragrance. A book can take you to faraway places-adventures that you dream about at night while you sleep.

I know that my love of reading came from my seventh-grade teacher, and I made sure when I began homeschooling my children that reading was an essential part of their learning. One year, I read over two hundred books to my children. I wanted to give them the passion to go places that I would never be able to take them. I wanted them to *feel* the words on the pages of a book and have them taken away by the story and the adventure it could take them to.

Reading changed my life, and my love for it enriched my life with possibilities I never would've imagined.

I haven't stopped reading. I've never stopped just taking a day to curl up with a good book until I'm lost in the pages, somewhere far away, and living a whole different reality.

Reading is a special key that can unlock doors to take you wherever you want to be. The treasure of reading didn't just get me

through my difficult times in middle school but
has gotten me through more painful events
than I can even count. God is good like that-
double dipping and intertwining those gifts for
more than just one moment.

He is *good*, gifting us with treasures that can
take our minds far from our reality in those
moments when we just need a break.

I have now read hundreds of books
throughout my lifetime that have ignited a spark
in me, healed me, transformed me, delivered
me, loved on me, captured me, and gave me a
deeper love for myself. Reading is a tool, and
my tool was also the gift that was given to me
from the foundations of my existence: given to
me for such a time as this.

Miss Ludwig

    As I think about the treasure that I found in my seventh-grade teacher, I can't help but mention another one of my teachers who also impacted me greatly.

    Miss Ludwig was never one to stay inside the confines of a box, so it was no surprise to see her standing outside of her pocket, rather than inside it like all the other treasures. She was my English Composition teacher, and we constantly butted heads. I'd find myself standing in the corner as punishment for talking in class or debating with her over every single topic. I had to sit in class with gum on my nose, because I refused to swallow it or not chew it in her class and everywhere else for that matter. It makes me chuckle thinking about it now, because not a day goes by that I don't have gum in my mouth as an adult.

The purpose of her class was to teach us how to think outside the box with creative writing. I loved writing; I loved her class and deep in my soul, I really did love her as a teacher. I didn't test her because I hated her; I tested her to see if she was real— to see if she could look past the brokenness I carried and see the girl beneath it.

We had writing assignments frequently, and she would critique them and then hand them back to the class for us to improve them. I hated the critiquing process, but I loved everything else about creative writing.

Once, my sister and I were mad at each other. I found my retaliation through putting love letters that her boyfriend had given her on every floor of the school. When she found out, she acted swiftly and stormed into my English class and poured perfume over my already greasy hair. We were only allowed to bathe and wash our hair once a week, so her revenge hurt and embarrassed me to the core. Miss Ludwig got between us, and she told me instead of finding a way to get even, I should write a story and put my feelings on paper. As I poured my heart out onto the paper in front of me, my fierce anger subsided, and although I was still upset, I could now write my feelings on paper instead of expressing them through physical force. I loved Miss Ludwig for that lesson she taught me.

Miss Ludwig wasn't anything pretty to look at.
She was awkward and seemed lonely to me.
She wore the same kind of blue dickie pants and a
sweater vest every day, but none of that mattered
to me, because she was helping me develop
writing skills that I would carry with me for the
rest of my life.

One assignment we were given required us to
think of a window and describe what we saw
outside it. I loved this assignment so much that
when I homeschooled my own children, I gave
them the same one. I chose to write about my
window. I wrote about sneaking out of the house
after getting my clothes ready earlier that day and
hiding them under the mattress of the bed. I was
afraid that Miss Ludwig would know it was me in
my story, but I was compelled to write it. I would
sneak out every night and walk down the street
and meet up with town guys. They would pick me
up and cruise around for a while, and I'd
eventually find myself in the back seats of their
cars trying to convince myself they were loving
me but knowing deep down that it really wasn't
love. I was a hurting young girl with nowhere to
go where I could feel safe.

Looking back over my life, there was no one
that loved *me* for *me*. I was used over and over
again and shamed because of the secrets that my
life held. I'd come back home feeling empty, get
into bed, and fall asleep only to get up and go to
school and do it all over again the next night.
When I handed in my story, I was a little afraid
but yet excited that I was able to form the words
and put my experiences in story form. The whole

class waited patiently for our papers to come back. When we received our papers back, my teacher asked me if I could meet her in her office after class. Nervous that she knew it was me my story was about, I walked hesitantly into her office. I was only able to relax when she started talking. She told me that I had a gift, that I was creative, and that I had an eloquent way of expressing my words. She said she felt the energy in my writing, and that if I kept up with it, I would someday be an author representing this school. I walked out of her office on the verge of tears, but I held them back not knowing if she was really right or if it was just a wistful dream.

Regardless, none of that mattered. All that mattered to me was that she believed in me. She acknowledged me and showed me love through her words. She saw something in me and gave me a reason to believe in myself. Miss Ludwig is no longer with us, but years ago before she passed, I saw her at my counselor's office. I'm not sure if we shared the same one, but I told Miss Ludwig how she impacted my life and that the words she spoke to me were life- changing. I wrote my first book forty years later, and I dedicated it to her. She gave me the tools I needed to develop my writing abilities, and I owe them to her.

The treasure of my English teacher—the teacher who thought outside the box, the teacher who believed in me—is a gift that continues to bless not just me, but others as I continue to write stories that impact people

everywhere. The gift she gave to me was a gift
that God knew I needed.

And so, my story began...

Amber Renee:
Little Flame Reborn

My father, Alfred, as a child.

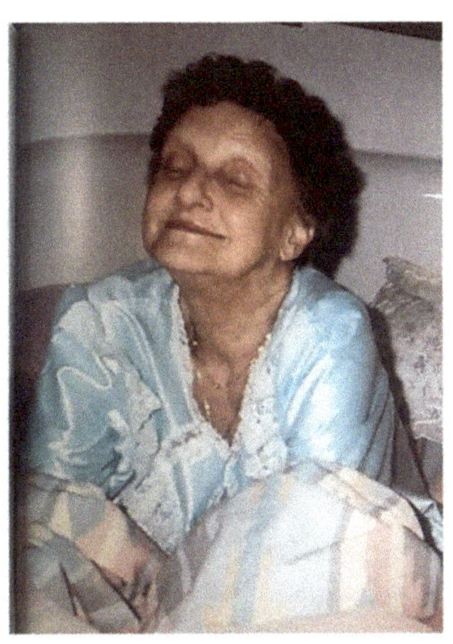

My sweet, sweet grandmother.

My father.

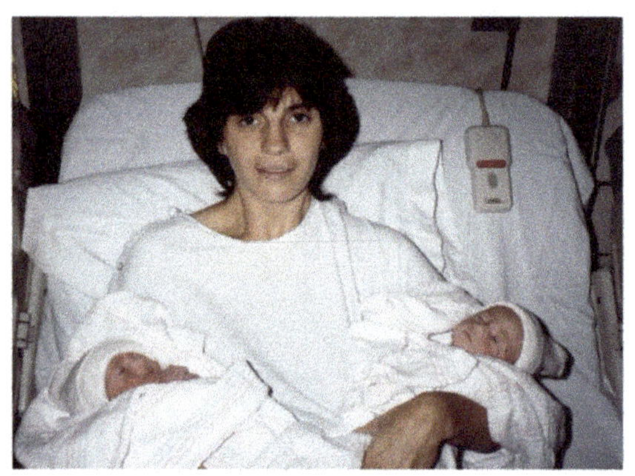

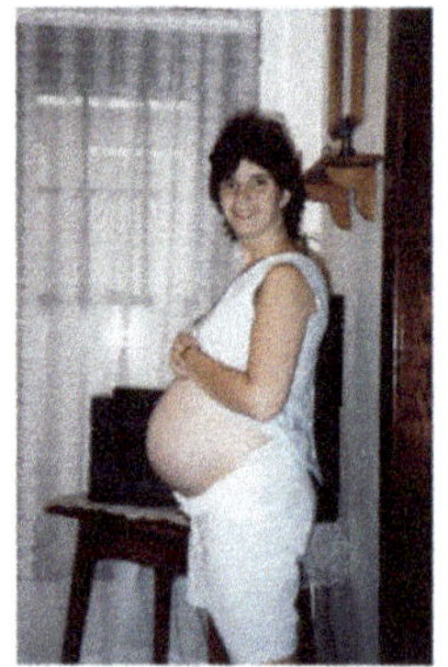

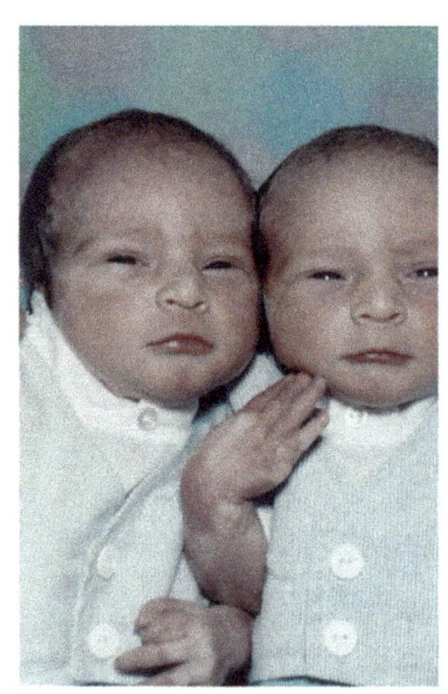

My double blessing:
my twin sons.

My dad with the twins.

The twins
with their great-grandparents.

TEXAS COWBOY
Hall of Fame
Fort Worth Stockyards

You made me a mom.
You saved me,
and there are no words
To describe how much you
mean to me.

There's no way to be
a perfect mother,
but there's a million ways
to be a good one.

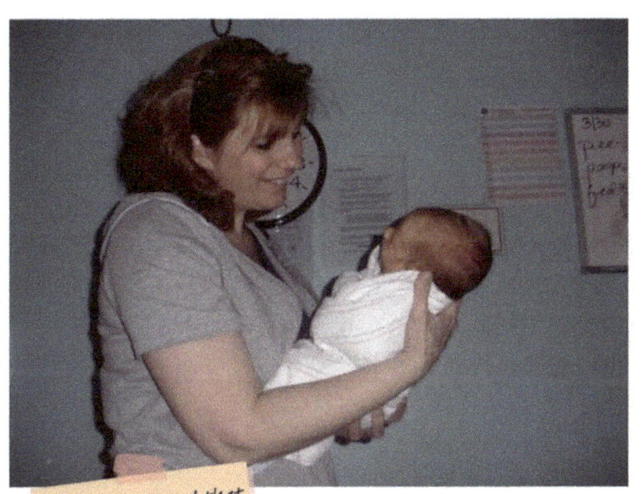

I turned 40, and that chapter of my life began with one of my greatest treasures: the first of my grandchildren.

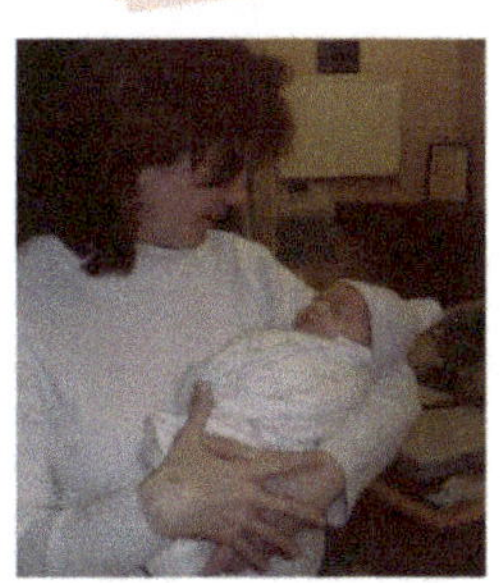

Scared? Good.

There is no growth inside your own comfort zone.

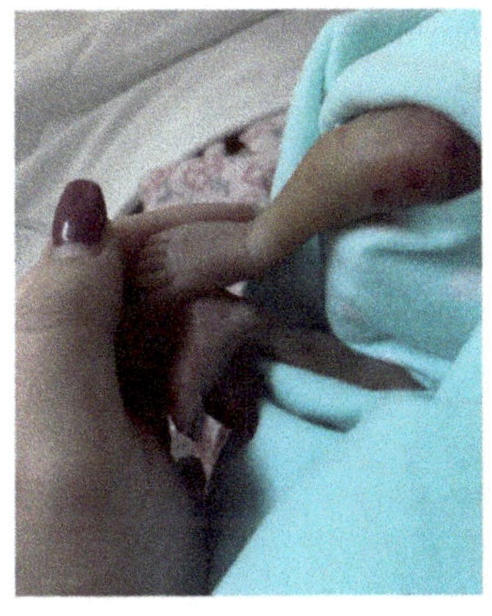

The moment
time stopped:
March 17th, 2019.

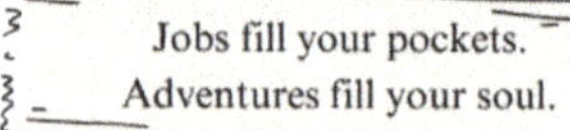
Jobs fill your pockets.
Adventures fill your soul.

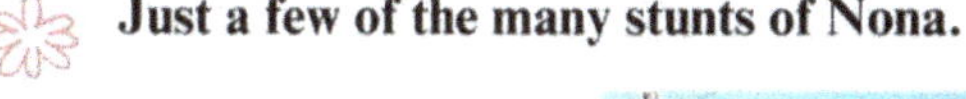

Just a few of the many stunts of Nona.

My first grandchild...
How fast they grow!

ARKANSAS
BRICK
ROAD

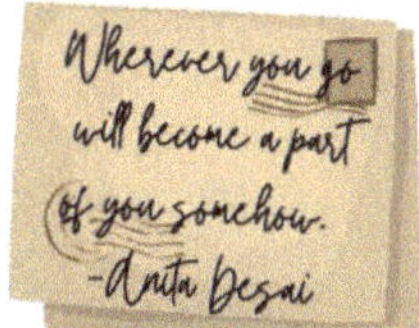
Wherever you go
will become a part
of you somehow.
—Anita Desai

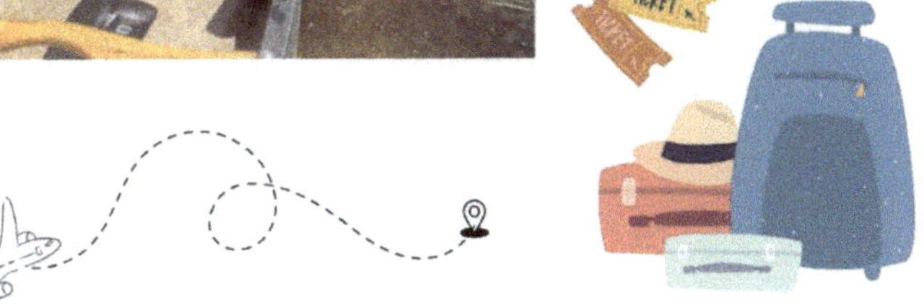
TICKET
TICKET

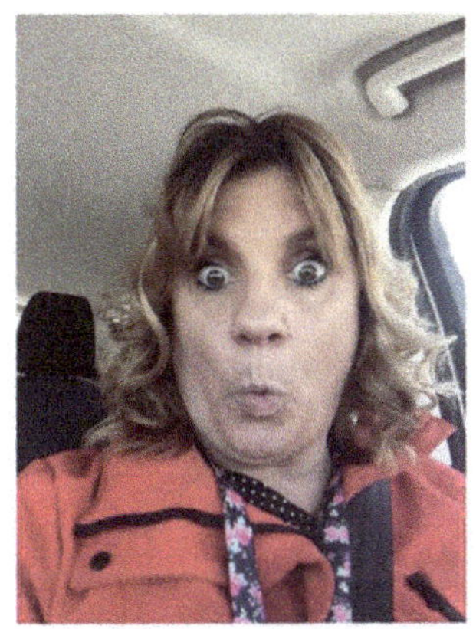

Driftwood Beach:

The place where I took the very first step of my journey toward becoming an author.

AND BEFORE I KNEW IT,
I WAS A PUBLISHED AUTHOR.

ONLY
THE STRONGEST
Women
BECOME
Writers

"The function of freedom is to free
someone else, and if you are no longer
wracked or in bondage to a person
or a way of life, tell your story.
Risk freeing someone."
Anne Lamott

The Bolsters

The next treasure I saw brought tears to my eyes as I reminisced on the depth of God's love and grace He'd given me through it. When I was around fourteen, I stopped attending the church I grew up in. A young girl in my youth group had gotten pregnant, and the youth leaders gathered us all for a meeting to discuss it. We were told that since she'd made an adult decision, she should associate with adults and was kicked out of the youth group.

I was taken aback and disturbed by the youth leaders' decision and consequently left the church. Where was the love in that? I didn't see Jesus in that. For all the grace and forgiveness that was emphasized, I didn't see it in their actions.

There was a church near my high school that was pastored by a Reverend Bolster. I began attending there, but it was so formal and different from what I'd grown up with. The Reverend even wore a robe. In addition to pastoring, Reverend Bolster had his hands full umpiring the girls' softball team I was forced to play on one year. He'd also gotten me a summer job working at the church daycare. I loved that job with all my heart. Once, journalists from a local newspaper came to interview some of the daycare employees and take pictures, and *my* picture ended up in the newspaper. I remember feeling so special that it was *my* picture in the article. Although I didn't attend that church for too long, the seeds that were planted during my time there would grow into something special just a few years later.

At sixteen, I was anything but in a great place. Overwhelmed and feeling hopeless, I decided my life wasn't important, and I wanted to end it. I stood on a bridge in my hometown, ready to jump. I just wanted it to stop hurting. I wanted the crushing pain I carried to end. Before I could jump, I was stopped by a police officer who brought me to a psychiatric center for children. There, I gave my life over to God after finding out I was pregnant. I was dumbfounded and confused by what was happening in my life. The center wouldn't release me into the environment I'd just come out of, so they somehow contacted the Bolsters to see if they had a safe place for me. I later found out that the police had actually gone to the Bolsters and told them where I was, and that's how they found out I was at the psychiatric center. Reverend Bolster said that they would house me. At the time, I didn't know that the Bolsters thought it was just for the weekend, or that it *wasn't* a semi-permanent place like I'd thought.

One of their daughters was in another country for a year as a foreign exchange student. They also had two other children at home, but still, they opened up their home to a very broken, pregnant teenage girl. They rented me a room for $50 a week, and I was allowed to use anything in their home. I even sat with them at dinner. It took me a while to feel like I mattered to them, but gradually that changed into a feeling of belonging.

I woke up each day in the quiet morning stillness and walked to a nearby McDonalds about a mile away, where I had gotten a job. My shift started at 6 o'clock sharp every morning, but I was always there on time despite the exhaustion that comes with pregnancy. The job gave me the money I needed to pay my rent, and I was grateful for it. Mrs. Bolster, who was scheduled to be out of town over my due date, found a nurse who was studying to work in labor and delivery to go with me to birth classes, as well as be with me in the delivery room when I had my baby. The nurse was a gentle woman in her early 40s, with kind eyes and hints of gray in her hair. Her mere presence was calming.

Still in awe of the little life I was carrying, I began decorating my room for my precious girl's arrival. I settled on a Disney theme, using the baby characters and Disney minis to create the perfect space to bring my sweet girl home to.

Not long before my due date, the Bolsters took me on their family outing to the Toronto Zoo. As we got settled in for the drive to the zoo, I made a snarky comment telling Reverend Bolster to roll the windows down until the air conditioning was cold enough to cool the car down. He chuckled and rolled the windows down for me. To this day he still rolls the windows down and waits a few minutes before turning the air conditioning on. Despite being exhausted from all the walking we did and barely being able to move the next day, I remember feeling like I *belonged.* To me, that outing will always be Jesus acting in human form.

Two days before my due date, I told my manager at McDonalds I wouldn't be returning to work, as I was about to have my baby. The next morning, I went into labor. Shortly after, I was gazing at the face of a beautiful little girl. *My beautiful little girl.* Navigating parenthood as a single young teen proved to be more challenging than I'd ever imagined. When I couldn't get my sweet girl to stop crying, Mrs. Bolster would come into my room and rock her in the rocking chair until *my* tears subsided. I knew then that I was more than just a girl renting a room. The Bolster's thought of me as a daughter. The compassion they showed me will always be dear to my heart. When I started dating my first husband, they even allowed him in their home to babysit my daughter while I worked my second job. The Bolsters were a lifeline for me. After I'd gotten married, they left the church and moved on to their next ministry, and we lost touch. Years later, we reconnected through social media and were able to meet up and have dinner together. Mrs. Bolster was able to stay at my house when I wasn't there, and I was able to visit them in New Hampshire where they lived.

I can never repay them for everything they did for me, but I *can* make sure I live my life with grace and selfless generosity, always having my door open for anyone who needs a place to stay and a meal for whoever is hungry.

I am forever grateful to the Bolsters for their love and for being Jesus in human form to a broken girl that continues even now on her journey to wholeness: a journey that started with a family that took me in. My heart is full of treasures, all special in their own way, and all of them played a part in my journey to wholeness.

Amber Renee

I didn't even need to see the next treasure; I could feel it. My heart was overwhelmed with emotion and a love I'd never experienced before. I looked closely, knowing that it was going to be my little girl all dressed in pink, and I wasn't disappointed when I was right.

That sweet girl was my saving grace. She came into my life at such a dark time, and as she did then, she continues to bring pure sunshine into my life.

I was a sixteen-year-old girl, broken, lost, and struggling to pick up the fragments of myself. My life was shattered into a million tiny pieces that all threatened to swallow me up. One evening, overwhelmed and alone, I gave up. I couldn't keep fighting like this. What was the point, anyway? I could never be whole again. What was I even fighting for? I found myself standing on a bridge, looking down into the darkness. One simple decision and I could put a stop to my failure, my pain, and all my brokenness. I longed for peace. No one would miss me if I was gone. Death was the only solution I could come up with.

I had just gotten back to my hometown after being in foster care where I'd been sent after speaking up about the sexual assault I'd experienced at the hand of my uncle. While there, I'd made a mistake, and instead of owning up to it with my foster care parents, I'd decided to run. I wish I could've gone back, but I carried so much shame for so many things, and I couldn't face them. I had no idea if they would forgive me and take me back. I know now they would have, but at that point in my life, I didn't know that kind of love even existed, and the only person that ever truly made me feel loved was my grandma.

Once I'd arrived back in town, I found myself walking the streets of my hometown and met up with a guy that I'd always thought of as good-looking. He flattered me, telling me I'd grown up into a beautiful girl. As we chatted, I mentioned not having a place to stay, and he wasted no time in offering his apartment. He shared the apartment with one of my friends and her boyfriend, so I agreed. What else was I going to say, since I had nowhere to go? I moved in, and at first, it was fun. Parties were happening constantly, and since my friend was there too, I felt safe. I did coke for the first and last time in my life. It didn't appeal to me.

My boyfriend had a girlfriend during the day, so I became his girlfriend for the night hours. I knew it was wrong and that it wasn't love, but I was caught up in the feeling of being wanted. The age difference was significant and early on I knew I was being groomed, but I told myself it was just his way of flirting. I knew I was being used, but I felt noticed, I felt pretty, and even though he was using me to get what he wanted, my love and attention-starved heart looked the other way.

I worked at McDonalds during the day and found random stuff to do after work because of his girlfriend. I knew there would be a breaking point for me, but I didn't know when and I never dreamed it would involve me deciding life was meaningless. I never would've imagined that a day would come when I decided *my* life held no value, but it did come. That brings me back to the bridge. It was going to be the end of all my pain: my saving grace.

My plan ended abruptly when I was pulled down by a police officer, restrained, and put in the back of a police car. He took me to a pediatric psych ward where I was inspected from head to toe, making sure I had no visible signs of self-harm. They drew labs, did physicals, and asked countless questions. I was angry. I was scared. Why couldn't they just leave me alone?

The next day, I was called to a bright office with floor-to-ceiling glass panels. A few nurses were gathered there as well as the doctor, who was looking over my file and slowly nodding.

"Did you know that you're pregnant?" The doctor kept talking but it was like he was speaking a foreign language because I couldn't understand anything past that question. Shocked and stunned, I tried to comprehend what was happening.

I was growing a baby inside me.

"Can I go back to my room?" My voice was small, shocked, and in awe. One of the nurses got up and took me back to my room. I fell to the ground and cried out to God, begging for his love to fall upon me. I told him He'd saved me and my baby, and I would honor him all the days of my life. I put my hand on my stomach, and for the first time in my life, I felt a love deeper than anything I'd ever imagined-a love that I had almost destroyed by taking my life. I made promises at that moment to the little being that was inside of me. I was a little shocked at how this child got here. I knew about the birds and the bees, but I thought that for a baby to be born, two people had to love each other so much that they each gave a part of themselves to the other because the love could only be experienced like that. I knew I didn't feel love, and I knew the father didn't love me.

The knowledge that a little life was growing in me gave me a new perspective on my own life, and I was going to do whatever it took to ensure this precious life would never endure any of the pain I'd had to live with. I was going to protect my baby from any kind of sadness. The doctor had said we could discuss 'options' regarding my pregnancy, but the only option I had was keeping my baby. At sixteen, I had no idea how God would do that, but I surrendered my life to Him, trusting that He'd work it out.

The first thing He did was find a family that would allow me to stay at their home. I had my job that would take me back, so 28 days later I was out of the center and starting a new life.

The beginning wasn't easy. I was bullied mercilessly, and as I walked home from work every day, girls would roll down their car windows just to yell that I was carrying a bastard child, and that I was lying about who the father was. I didn't care what they said, because I had a life inside me, and I was going to do everything and anything to take care of this baby. I found out I was having a baby girl, and although in my heart I already knew, to have it confirmed was the best feeling. Now, I could give her a name. *Amber Renee: little flame reborn.* God saved me and gave my spark back, and I wanted her to know that even in her name, she was special.

For all these years, we have been on a journey together. I had to grow up fast. Becoming a mom at seventeen wasn't easy, but every time I look at her even now I well up with so much emotion and love for her. She is a remarkable woman and has become my true best friend. We don't always see eye to eye, but whatever happens, we always come back to each other and feel that bond we share together. Life has never been easy for her and she's had some hard times, but every time she falls, she gets back up. She hasn't always received the love she deserves, she's experienced heartache in relationships and in her health, but she always takes a moment, gets back up, and keeps pushing forward. I wonder where she got that from? I've spent a lot of time regretting some decisions I've made in my life that have affected my children, but I will never regret saying yes to her. I've never questioned if I made the right choice in keeping her. I'll never regret the sacrifices that I made for her, and how I stood up for her when no one else did. She didn't ask to be born to a hurting young teen. My choices, though not her fault, have affected her greatly, but not once has she ever hated me or said anything mean to me about the choice I made to keep her.

This treasure has done more for me than any other treasure. They all have been important to my healing, but she was and is the most significant. God took my shambled heart and chose to heal it with a little girl named Amber Renee. Little flame reborn. The greatest treasures come in small packages, sometimes with little bows and pink dresses.

The Church Steeple

I hesitate to write about the next treasure I saw within the pockets of my heart. For so long I thought this was a precious treasure. It was—until it wasn't. The church steeple peeked out of its pocket, like it was almost hesitant.

For as long as I could remember, church had been a safe haven for me. It's where I learned about the love of Jesus, and where I saw people that didn't just *have* faith but lived it out on a daily basis. I experienced friendships that lasted far beyond my time in church, and it wasn't just friends I found, but family. After being estranged from my biological family, my church family made me feel like I belonged. I found peace within the walls of the church building. I grew in those pews, and I cried out at the altar. I met God in ways I never would've anywhere else. I raised my children in those pews with the church helping me through Sunday school, vacation Bible school, and youth group. My children honed their talents, singing in front of church and reciting Bible verses to whoever would listen. I sat through classes, ladies' Bible studies, sat under great preaching, and eventually I taught classes, held Bible studies for the women, and preached from the pulpit many times. I had visions and dreams and gave out of my need and heart. I served the church because it was home. It was my family. I sought out women for their wisdom, aspiring to follow Titus 2, with the older women teaching the younger. I wanted to be just like them and have their hunger for God and truth. I was always searching for more of God's love, to experience His peace and to be accepted and protected. Jesus saved me, and I wanted Him to see, though my life and actions, that I was forever grateful for His love for me in sending His Son to save my soul. Jesus was and is everything to me. His love was more than I could comprehend, knowing I'd been lost, and He found me, that I'd been blind, but He gave me eyes to see.

Within the walls of my home, behind closed doors and in secret, I was leading a drastically different life. I didn't have the love and the family that I had at church, but rather now-exes, one after the other, that hurt me through infidelity and domestic abuse. I ran to the church and its leaders, only to be told that if I was better at submitting, better at praying, and better at showing love to my husbands, these things would have never happened. They told me that ending the abuse was my responsibility, that I needed to be silent, and that I should let my husband win without saying a word. I was told never to deny sex, because that was spiritual warfare. I was left alone with no help when my abusive ex finally left. One of the pastors came to my home, talked to my daughters about the abuse that was happening, and said that someday I would be safe; someday the secret would come out. After that, he got in his car and drove away as if it was nothing. I gave training tapes to the pastors on domestic violence, just to have them set on a shelf out of sight, never to be touched. I taught at ladies' luncheons, focusing on sexual abuse, and found that it was happening right under our noses, and we swept it under the rug. I've had men who had promised to be there for my sons tell me if I'd just submitted more, I wouldn't being raising my children alone, and then tell their wives not to hang out with me because I'd be a bad influence.

How do you sit in the church pews, knowing a woman is getting abused and still say nothing? How do you justify that behavior? *How do you claim to love like Jesus but look the other way in that situation?*

When I went through my second divorce, I looked around the church building and found no one that I would want to have shepherd my sons into manhood. I walked away from the church in tears, reeling from a pain so intense that I have yet to return. With a new perspective on the outside, I began to see the dysfunction, to see how protected the sins were of others in the church, how some got help, and how others were dying inside, putting on a happy face because there was no safety in telling the truth. I saw people protect the abusers and defend them because they needed them for their bowling leagues or needed their talent on a worship team, or perhaps just needed the money they brought into the church. I saw victims *not* being protected, and I heard stories of abuse in nurseries, pastors' offices, and closets in the church. I've heard broken women disclose the abuse they endured at their husbands' hands, seen children that bore the marks of the failures of their parents-the same parents who focused everything on their leadership for the church family, while their own families were left broken with nowhere to go.

My faith in Jesus never has faltered. I am so thankful for his love despite the pain I endured in those circles. I am so grateful for the people he led into my life, the ones who anchored me, keeping me from drowning. I'm blessed by the friends who understood why I left and gave me space to continue to heal and to feel safe. I live in awe of God's love for me, mind blown at His unconditional love and understanding in spite of my humanity. My quiet times with Him have never failed to lead me to His throne room of mercy and grace. He's carried me through some of the most difficult times I've had at church. He gave me a voice when the world around me was silent. Most of all, He understood when I couldn't do it anymore.

My time at the altar—my time at His feet—still overwhelms my heart with gratitude for the lessons I learned. I'm so grateful that I had a safe haven in the church for a while: a place I felt I belonged.

Even in the here and now, God continues to lead me to a church without walls-one that exists within the homes I go to, the stores I visit, and the people I meet every day. I am still changing lives for Jesus. Perhaps my work isn't within a church building, but it *is* where people need it the most: on the streets and in the homes, where not even the traditional 'churchgoers' would venture; where Jesus is most needed but rarely found.

The steeple I saw in my heart's pocket so many years ago holds countless memories, but that treasure, the steeple, has been replaced with the cross, and in that cross, I have found an even greater treasure. At the foot of the cross, where my tears have washed the feet of Jesus; He has picked me up and made me whole. The change in my treasure—from a steeple to the cross—will forever make me smile.

The Stack of Books

A stack of books sticking out of one of my heart's pockets could only mean one thing. A huge smile spread over my face, because I knew that stack of books represented my years of homeschooling.

Homeschooling my children was and will always be my single greatest accomplishment in life. To take the minds of my children and gently help mold and shape them into the people they'd grow up to be, to be able to pour into their little minds; it is by far a most cherished treasure.

How could a girl with so little education guide the development of her children's minds and teach them everything they'd need to flourish in life after they'd left home? How could a mom with only a GED be capable enough to handle such a large responsibility? How did I teach them to read and write? How did I venture outside my comfort zone to bring education to the most important people in my life? The only logical answer is God. None of it could've happened without Him.

When my eldest daughter turned four, her dad and I began discussing the options we had for her education. He'd attended a Christian school from K-12, and he was adamant that our daughter would not follow the same route. I'd attended public school and didn't feel strongly towards one way or the other. However, just the thought of putting my little girl on a bus each day tore me apart. The realization that sending her to school would mean being away from my daughter during the day for the entirety of the school year left me in turmoil. The thought of it was unbearable. The only thing I could do was pray, and pray I did, begging God for directions and for answers.

One night not long after, I had a vivid dream. In my dream, I was standing at the bus stop with the other mothers and their children, waiting for the bus to arrive. It rolled slowly to a stop, and the doors opened. One by one, the children let go of their mother's hands and disappeared inside the bus. I stepped up with my daughter, and just as I was about to let her go, the bus doors abruptly closed and across them in bold letters was written the word, NO. The bus left just as quickly as it had come, and I woke, startled, not entirely sure where I was for a moment. I woke my husband who'd been sound asleep next to me and told him what I'd just dreamed. I felt it was

God's way of telling us we were to homeschool. I felt *peace,* and I finally had an answer.

Just twenty-one years old with two other toddlers and one on the way, I had no idea *how* I was going to do this, but I knew I'd find a way. I knew this was my answer. My load of responsibility was already heavy, but I was up for the challenge.

I dove headfirst into anything and everything I could find on the topic of homeschooling. I searched for mentors: people that could lead and guide my first steps as I learned all about the journey that it would be. I soaked up every bit of information that I could, knowing this was something I wasn't just going to do, but something I was going to do *well*.

With no idea that this dream would take me 27 years to complete, I dug in and gave it everything I had. Despite the struggles I faced, they were some of the best years of my life. From marriage struggles, infidelity, divorce, and abuse, to navigating life as a single mother, poverty, and pain from which I desperately tried to shield my children, those were my saving years. *My grace years.*

When life came at me in a fury, I found peace and stability in sitting around the table with my children answering math questions, explaining the contradictory grammar rules for the hundredth time, because let's be real—they really *don't* make sense—the many books I read aloud, the unit studies I designed for them, and the joy of watching their little faces light up when they aced a test. If asked, some of my children would tell you they hated being homeschooled, but others would say it was good. To some of them, I was selfish. To the others, I was selfless and saved them. To a few of them, I ruined them, and the others would tell you I prepared them for the real world. I know I did the right thing, regardless, and the memories I made with them are some of my fondest. Homeschooling was the one stable thing I had, and it gave me hope throughout the challenges of those years.

The opportunities my children had due to homeschooling were endless. As long as they got their work done, it didn't matter if they were finished by mid-morning or if they'd done extra the day before so they would have more free time on any given day. Because of the flexibility, we were able to dive into topics that public school would've barely brushed the surface of. We did crafts, watched videos, went on field trips, and had countless other adventures. We even had the opportunity to take a covered wagon ride. My daughters and I baked for the homeless shelter and spent the evenings doing crafts and singing. One year, the twins and I made one hundred hats for the homeless. At the age of 14, the boys were also able to apprentice with different businesses and learned the basics of electrical work, roofing, and remodeling.

My own education was limited. I know I didn't teach everything right, and sometimes my children came to me with questions I couldn't answer. I didn't always know what the books were talking about. I utilized tutors and other classes to help teach the things I couldn't.

As I look at my children now, grown and with families of their own, I see the results of my effort in the things they have and continue to accomplish. My heart swells with pride in knowing that I played such a role in creating the people they are today.

There are days when tears flood my eyes knowing that maybe homeschooling wasn't the best choice for all my children—every child has different needs—and I wonder who they'd be if I hadn't made the choice I did. Even when I do feel that way, my sons will come to me, reassuring me that if I obeyed God and listened to His voice, then I have nothing to worry about. I did what He told me to do, and the rest of it is in His hands.27 years of gently shaping and guiding the minds of the next generation...my years of growing, learning not just with my children, but learning who *I* was—the person I was meant to be. 27 years of peeling back the layers of myself that I'd grown in a desperate attempt to protect my fragile heart, of learning what true sacrifice was, and of thanking God for giving me such clear direction in the dream I had so many years ago.

In the darkest moments and the most brutal storms, God gave me an anchor; a lifeboat, so to speak. He gave me a passion for learning and the ability to pass it on to my greatest loves: my six children.

Thinking of that stack of books brings tears to my eyes, and I'll eternally be grateful for that treasure: a reminder of the years when, despite the storms, I never gave up.

My Friends

Looking into my heart once more, there was no way I could miss the people jumping up and down in one of the pockets, their laughter echoing happiness throughout my heart. There was no mistaking that it was my friends I was seeing as part of the treasure that God planted inside my heart. Each one of them brought a special feeling throughout my heart, and down to my very core, I knew I never could have survived life without them. I became a better person because of their love and faith in me. These people were my family, my saving grace, and the ones who made me feel like I belonged. Each of them taught me lessons in life that continue to impact me today.

As I looked at each dear face, memories flooded my heart. I could pinpoint the moments when we'd become friends and even family. From the time I was just a child up until I was grown, these were the ones that taught me to survive, to get back up when you get knocked down, and no matter what you're facing, to just put one foot in front of the other. These were the ones that, when it was vacant, filled the role of mother, sister, and whatever else I needed. These were the ones who let Jesus work through them in such a way that it was as if it *was* Jesus with me; Jesus in human form.

Some of them were dear childhood friends who knew my pain, my secrets, the shame I carried but never judged me for any of it, and cherished our friendship just as I did. They knew more than they let on, but believed in me just the same. They lifted me up in times of heartache and wiped my tears when my marriage fell to pieces over infidelity. They were my shoulder to cry on when I faced domestic violence, my hand to hold through brutal divorces, and my support and rock as I navigated single parenthood.

When I hurt my knee playing tennis, it was one of those sweet friends that carried me up the hill so I could go home, and the next day, dragged me downstairs and out to her van to take me to the hospital where I found out my knee was broken in several different places.

After a burn injury left me unable to keep up with my children and myself, these were the friends who came and took care of the things I couldn't. I hadn't known them for long, but they stepped up without so much as a second thought and showered me in love.

When I'd sat in the dark, tears streaming down my face as I tried to understand how my husband could just walk away from me and our daughters for the third time, a woman had shown up at my door, a plate of warm chocolate chip cookies in hand, just to tell me she'd be there if I needed anything. We became close friends, and still are today. These friends were the ones who cried *with* me, as I battled the decision to marry someone my heart knew wasn't the right one, telling myself that it would help relieve my burden of shame.

I was blessed with neighbors who turned into friends and became surrogate parents to my children. I always felt as if I had family living next door.

When I struggled to make ends meet as a single mom, they filled my freezer and cupboards. When I was without a car, they gifted me one so I could take my children back and forth to wherever they needed to go. They were essential to my homeschooling career. We'd meet, share ideas, books, and techniques to help our children grasp difficult concepts. My children spent countless hours with the other moms and their children over the years, learning the things I couldn't teach.

My friends were the ones who made sure my birthday was special and that I received Christmas gifts, and when I had nowhere to go during the holidays, they'd welcome me into their homes with open arms.

We did Bible studies around my table and at churches, praying together for a miracle for our husbands and families. If I called in the middle of the night, these were the friends that would answer. When my life felt like it was falling apart, rather than judge me, they let me sit with the pain and held me until I accepted God's truth. They'd never allow me to feel alone, especially in the darkest seasons of my life.

Some friends are only meant to be in your life for a season, and I've been blessed with sweet people who were there at just the right time but had other paths to follow. Some friends walked away for other reasons: some had husbands who thought I was a bad influence, others disagreed with my political views, and for some, our interests simply changed and we drifted apart.

The friends who stayed for the long haul? They're my lifeline. When I start to lose hope, they're there to encourage me. We can live our lives and not talk for months, but one phone call and it's like not even a day has passed.

We joke and laugh and cry together, smudging teary makeup onto each other's teary makeup on each other's shoulders. We've helped raise each other's children, and now we're watching our children raise *their* children.

Life is better with a circle of people around you who may not share your DNA, but rather share your heart. They'll help mold and form you, and whenever you're apart, you're longing for the moment you'll be back together again, continuing to make a lifetime of memories together.

No one is born with a fan club, but when God gives you *your* people, they'll be your VIP, all holding backstage passes for life.

God didn't leave anything out with that treasure. My friends came in all shapes and sizes, all different ages, and all different walks of life, but together, we've created a club that I am thrilled to be a part of. I am eternally grateful we were all willing to join together, and in doing so, create one of my greatest treasures.

The Twins

The next treasure I saw in one of my heart's
pockets overwhelmed me with joy and gratitude.
Two little bundles of pure love, two little blue
outfits, two little boys, one with his thumb in his
mouth, and the other with his two fingers: my
identical twin sons.

There is no way I could ever verbalize the
emotion that floods my heart when I think about
the joy they've brought to me. I never wanted
sons and every time I got pregnant, I desperately
prayed that the baby growing in my womb would
be a darling little girl. I was terrified of raising
sons. What if they grew up and hurt women like
I'd been hurt? As a mother, I could never handle
that kind of pain. After all, I was still healing
from and grieving the cruelty and brokenness I'd
experienced at the hands of men, and I had a lot

of healing left before I could even *think* about having a son.

God knew my heart, as well as my past, and He loved me enough to honor that prayer for my first four pregnancies. When my first husband left for the third time, I had a dream that I had twin sons. I woke, startled, and then laughed. *There's no way that will ever happen.* My husband had just gotten a vasectomy, anyway, and now he'd gone and left me and my daughters. I brushed it off—it was just a dream—and it was never going to happen.

Shortly after, I found myself pregnant *and* unmarried. At the time, I was teaching a girls' class at church, and the guilt and shame I carried over getting pregnant out of wedlock drove me to the point where I considered terminating my pregnancy. After all, no one would ever know, and I'd carry that secret to the grave. Something stopped me. There was no way I could simply end my pregnancy. Little did I know that even if I had chosen to have an abortion, only one baby would've lost their life, leaving behind their twin sibling whose existence was yet to be discovered by me.

Despite the shame, judgmental looks, and the cruel whispering happening behind my back, I accepted my mistake. I held my head high. This was the consequence of my sin, the result of the choices *I* had made. I had no choice but to accept it.

Although I kept my secret until I was positive I was carrying a child, between the violent nausea, vomiting, being up all night writhing in pain

from the cramping and crawling to the bathroom
hoping for a moment of relief, I knew in my
heart what was happening. Exhausted and tired
of being sick, I made my way to the drugstore to
confirm what I already knew: I had life growing
inside me. With that knowledge, the very first
thing I did was go to the beach. I sat by the water,
listening to the gentle lapping of the waves.
Weighed down with shame, I wept. I knew I'd
disappointed my Heavenly Father. I cried out to
God, begging Him for forgiveness. I would've
never guessed that God would choose to bless me
with a child when there were so many other
deserving women, but despite all my failures and
shortcomings, He *did* choose me.

I reminded God of the deal we had regarding
my having a son, but before I even finished, I felt
love flow through my heart, and in that instant, I
knew I was carrying a boy. I promised God then
and there that I would raise my son to love,
honor, and trust God, to live a life of integrity,
and that I would do the best I knew know to raise
him to be a man of character. I promised God I
would show my son His grace and mercy, and
teach him that in spite of inevitable failures,
God's forgiveness and love knows no bounds. I
promised God that this little boy was His, and I
would do my best to remind him of that every
day.

I knew what I had to do next, and as much as I
didn't want to, I couldn't avoid it. Not only did I
have to tell the father, but I also had to explain
my failures to my precious daughters. Yes, I had
failed God, but I'd failed them as well. I prayed

God would redeem my failures and show my daughters His love despite my mistakes. When I broke the news to the father, he bluntly replied he had no intention of ever marrying me, but that when the baby was born, we'd go to court and split custody. Although shocked and disappointed, I knew I had made my own choices, and I was responsible for this little person growing inside me.

My next step was telling my sweet girls. When I broke the news to them, I received an understandably different response from each of my daughters. From one daughter, it was simply, "Mom, I'm praying for twins!" One of my daughters made it clear she felt let down and I was a hypocrite in her eyes. My oldest daughter was quiet for a second, and then looked up at me. "Does your body know you got divorced?" She queried. Without waiting for an answer, she continued, "Mom, no wonder you had sex. No one told your body you're not married anymore!" Her childish innocence warmed my heart, bringing a smile to my face.

I did my best to understand each feeling and emotion they had, as well as make sure each emotion and feeling was validated. After all, they had every right to their own reaction to the news. After I'd told my children, I made an appointment with the pastor of the church we were attending to explain that I was going to step down from teaching and being an usher. Although it was the last thing I would've intentionally done, I knew there was a chance that I would be a stumbling block to any child, and I had to take measures against that. The pastor listened to me explain everything, and when I was through, he put his hand on mine and looked at me.

"Bambi, if anyone says anything to you or gives you any problems, come to me," he said gently. His kindness meant the world to me. Fellow churchgoers had sent a few letters spewing hate, telling me I'd ruined my testimony and that their daughters would no longer be allowed around me.

One of my sweet friends who is up with Jesus now cupped my face gently in her hands and reminded me that the God we serve is a loving God, and that instead of looking at me in judgement, He chose to shower me with grace.

Shortly after telling my family and church family, I made an OB/GYN appointment. As I walked into the office, a sign saying something about twins caught my eye. I asked my doctor just for information on it, and she informed me that she would do an early ultrasound just to rule it out, but she wasn't concerned, and it was just a precaution.

At this point, the father had decided that we'd do this together, and somehow make it work. We had a dinner planned for that evening to reveal the gender of the baby together. Although I already knew in my heart that it was a boy, I asked the ultrasound tech to put the sex of the baby in an envelope so the father and I could open it together. While I was taken to an ultrasound room, the girls sat and waited in the waiting room. I lay down on the bed, and the ultrasound tech tilted her screen, grabbed the wand, and began moving it around my belly. As she was looking at measurements, she asked if twins ran in my family. I shook my head, trying to see the screen. She tilted it toward me, and I saw two babies nestled in my womb, one on top of the other. "Well, they run in your family now." She smiled. She went on to explain that there were, obviously, two babies and that they were identical twin boys. I can't even find adequate words for what went through my mind in that moment. It was a whirl of bewilderment, fear, worry, excitement, and I laughed and cried, wondering how on earth I'd tell the father. I remembered my daughter's prayer for twins, and pondered just how this would affect her trust in God and strengthen her belief that He *does* answer us. I thought about the nursey and all the baby things we needed. I was a single mom, and my income was very limited. The tech adjusted the doppler so that one baby was hiding when the girls came into the room, but the moment they looked up and at the black and white sonogram, one of the babies moved their foot. The girls' eyes lit up, and they smiled. "It looks like twins," one said excitedly. I couldn't wait for them to know. It was then that I remembered my dream from years ago, and realized wasn't *my* dream; it was God's blessing. Nothing could've prepared me for the years of being a mom to my two sons: my double blessing. I constantly corrected people when they'd say something about 'double trouble'. I never allowed anyone to shorten their names either. I'd chosen their names because of the meanings: Jehovah redeemed, and Jehovah established, and I wanted it to always be at the forefront of their lives.

I read to them at night, slowly rocking in the rocking chair, rubbing my belly. I sang Bible songs to them and read the stories of their namesakes. I prayed over their lives constantly, reminding God of the deal we had that these precious boys would grow up to love and honor Him.

When their dad found out that we were having twins, he didn't take the news very well, and when we went to dinner later, he ignored me. He didn't open the door and help me out of the car, or even wait for me. Instead, he walked ahead into the restaurant, his coldness visible in his clenched jaw. As we ate, although I already had both names chosen, he told me he was changing one of the middle names, and so to avoid an argument in the middle of the restaurant, I agreed. We finished dinner and he drove me home, but for the next few weeks, he stayed away from me.

The relationship was always full of ultimatums, and I often just went along with things because I didn't want to split custody of my sons. His temper and lifestyle were not something I wanted to influence the twins, but I knew God would do something to make sure my sons grew up to honor Him, and if it required sacrifice on my part, I was more than willing.

Life was never easy for the twins or my daughters, but the boys never lacked love. Their big sisters showered them with almost motherly love and devotion, more than fulfilling the sister role that they held. The twins were a blessing to all of us, and we did our best to protect them from any kind of harm. If anyone wanted to even get near them, they'd have to go through my daughters and me.

The boys' father and I did eventually marry, but it was never a loving relationship. It didn't take long for the abuse to start and reinforce my knowledge that my husband didn't love me. Although the marriage didn't last, I did stay long enough for my sons to be old enough to talk to the judges. My decisions back then have been questioned, but I had promised God that I would raise my sons with integrity and character. I'd promised Him I'd teach them how a man was to lay down their lives for their wives. From the time I first knew they existed up until they were grown, I spent my days praying over them, speaking truth into their lives. I'd made a decision to protect my sons. I couldn't sit back and let them witness firsthand the domestic abuse I suffered at the hand of their dad. I didn't want them to see their father hitting me, yelling at me, and telling me I was nothing, and them thinking that it was okay, or even normal.

When the boys' father filed for divorce, I made sure my sons were protected. The court saw right through their dad and granted me full custody. He'd never see my sons in person. The court had witnessed two years of him trying to get his way regardless of the cost, his poor methods of handling conflict, and his lack of love and care. I had to stay out of that part due to the court's recommendations.

I have no regrets. He made his choices, and I made mine. My choices revolved around the protection of my sons' hearts. His choices were made based on what he wanted when he wanted it, and he refused guidance from anyone. I was willing to do anything the courts asked because my sons' future hung in the balance. On the other hand, he was not about to do anything just because the court wanted him to.

I just knew I had a job to do, and I had a promise to keep in bringing up these boys to honor and please God. Everything I did for them was with that mission in mind. Every activity we did was to develop a characteristic or trait that they could bring to the table when they met the woman of their dreams. I know some may wonder how I could even accomplish that on a poverty budget, but the twins were my double blessing, and perhaps even a last-ditch effort to show God I was worthy enough to be their mom. I struggled so much with being a failure that at times I smothered them.

I fought my own demons that were trying to convince me I wasn't adequate to even have these boys in my life or call myself their mother. We went to church, and I taught them to stand up for the truth even if someone older in the room was teaching. I then walked away from the church building because I couldn't find a man I could trust with my sons' hearts. We had church at home where I taught them to look up the truth for themselves, to search out who God said they were, and not to believe something because someone says it's true. I'd come home to them sitting at the table with their open Bibles, devouring the word of God with Strong's Concordance and a thesaurus in hand, looking up the meanings of different verses. I loved their passion and heart for the Lord, but I also could see fear. I know some of it was the pressure I put on them to be genuine in their faith and always know how to represent Christ wherever they went.

I loved those boys so much, and we always had the best time together. We went on a lot of adventures, and I tried to say no to them as little as possible so that when I did have to say it, they'd know my answer was final. I spent hours reading with them and watching different TV shows in my room. I gave them more freedom than I was able to give their sisters just because I truly trusted them. They were leaders in our neighborhood; the other kids looked up to them. They'd go play basketball at the town park, where whoever was playing was more than happy to let them into the game. They helped business owners with odd jobs and were highly sought after because they could be trusted to follow through and get the job done. Whenever someone in the neighborhood needed help, they were right there, ready to lend a hand. They respected others and earned respect in return. Their laugh was contagious—the kind that makes your belly hurt. They loved pranks, planning kidnappings for fun, calling random people on the phone just for a reaction, and making people laugh with all their shenanigans. They were the life of the party, but at the same time were careful never to misrepresent themselves or **dishonor their name.**

Their lifelong desire was to join the military and so from an early age I tried my best to prepare them for it. From the time they were small, they were obsessed with G.I Joes and had over 100 of them. They spent hours upon hours playing with their miniature army men. When they were older, the G.I Joe 'wars' turned to airsoft wars with their friends and they'd be gone for hours at a time, completely immersed in whatever they were playing in the woods. There was an army surplus store not far from our home, and the boys and I would frequently go there so they could buy uniforms and other miscellaneous items for their airsoft wars. They played army with the neighborhood boys, making their own bootcamp and spending hours and hours pretending. I had them join a group that would kickstart their careers once they were old enough to join. I went to the recruiter's office periodically, just to make sure we were on the right path. The military was their dream, and as their mom, I didn't want to mess anything up that could hinder that goal or cause them to have to choose a different career entirely. I spent all those years preparing for the day they would leave for the military, thinking it would help me have an easier time, but nothing could be further from the truth. Nothing could've taken away the pain that was in my heart when they left. Nothing could've prepared me for the loss I experienced. Even writing it now brings tears to my eyes. I prepared them to leave and did everything I could to equip them for the next chapter of their lives, but no one and nothing could've prepared *me*. The only comparable pain I'd ever experienced was what I went through when my daughters left to go live with their dad.

The day my boys left, it finally hit me. They were grown. They were moving on, and I was left standing still. My feet didn't *want* to go to the next chapter of my life. I looked at the empty house and wanted to take back what I said about them going into the military at seventeen. I wanted one more moment with them. One more dinner spent laughing over their jokes. I wanted to walk into the dining room and see them at the table, studying the Word of God. They were my pride and joy and I invested in them from the very beginning to make this moment possible for them, but now I wanted to go back to the beach and take back what I promised God.

The next few years were difficult for me. I still struggle at times, not having them around. Each time they came home to visit, the goodbyes were never enough. I think what made it even more intense was that their leaving ushered in the empty nest stage of my life, and I had nothing to distract me from it.

They're both married now with families of their own, and I am no longer first in their lives. I knew my job as a mother, nurturing and guiding, was over when they left, but it's a job I never wanted to give up or end. Their lives are both full and my place in all of it is just to be in their corners. I cheer them on from the sidelines and they know my love is something they can trust in.

Parents and especially single parents don't have it easy. Raising a child so they can thrive as an adult is difficult on its own, but even more so when you have no one to lean on. I took my role seriously, and sometimes to my own detriment. I still need to be reminded that I did my part, and the rest is up to God. These are God's children and He simply loaned them to me for a moment. My job was to teach them and to throw them out of the nest so they could learn to fly. Both of them leaned not just to fly, but to soar above the mountains, taking in the magical view before them. The world is theirs for the taking, and they're doing a great job of finding their own ways.

My sons are a great treasure and I have reaped abundantly from the seeds that I planted. I am so grateful and so blessed to be called their mom. I can't thank God enough for the treasure that He placed in my heart in that of my double portion, and my double blessing.

My Grandchildren

The giggles and noise coming from the next pocket of my heart made me smile instantly. As I looked closer, I saw children bouncing around, picking their noses, and squabbling as they tried to get the gum I'd given them out of their hair. One was taking his diaper off while another two were fighting over a truck. Chaotic? Perhaps, but still the most beautiful chaos I'd ever seen. A treasure like this one will fill your heart till it bubbles over. I knew immediately that it was the little people that call me *Nona*.

I became a Nona at forty years old; it was the first big thing that happened when I entered the promised land after my fortieth birthday. When I held my first grandchild for the first time, I knew I was given a piece of heaven that would forever change the capacity of my heart. I didn't know that you could feel such overwhelming love for a little person that you met seconds ago.

My daughter Amber gave me my first grandchild, and I was able to be in the room with her as she labored for my grandson. I saw my daughter in the most pain I'd ever seen and even though I knew it was for a purpose, it was hard to see her hurting like that. I sang in her ear and encouraged her to keep pushing forward. I wanted to meet this little being that was going to change my life forever. Despite the long, intense labor, she ended up requiring an emergency C-section. I sat, defeated, in the waiting room. I felt robbed of this chance to watch my first grandson be birthed into this world. Regardless, I was the first person she asked for when she arrived back at her room. When I was introduced to my grandson, heard his name, and saw his tiny, perfect face, I was speechless. From that moment on, my little Isaiah changed and continues to change me in the best way possible.

As I write this, I have been blessed with an additional twelve grandchildren—thirteen in total. I know that this is not the end, and there are more coming to capture my heart. I love every moment I spend with them, and all the little dates we've had and will have. I've gone on trips with them and shared some magical moments that only a Nona could. That title carries such a powerful responsibility in loving them with hugs and kisses and being there in ways that parents aren't. Grandparents hold such a special position and play a unique role in the lives of their grandchildren.

I've experienced loss and heartache as a Nona. My grandchildren keep me alive; they make me feel wanted, and consequently, the loss of some of those relationships has been devastating. One of the first deaths I have mourned was that of my grandson, Isaac Joseph. I didn't think pain like that was even possible. *A child I was never able to hold. A child that would never call my name.* I'd never run around with him on the floor, or sneak treats to him while his parents weren't looking. I'd never be able to buy him Christmas gifts—you know, the annoying ones that make all the noise that'll drive the parents insane. On the day that he was born, a few hours after he'd made his entrance into the world, I received a FaceTime call from his mama. Although I was never able to meet him in person, on that call she showed my grandson to me from his head all the way down to his comically large feet. This past year I felt the need to visit him, so I gathered a few things and drove to the cemetery where he is buried. It's a beautiful place; majestic trees towering over the landscape, geese wandering through the lush grass, and the gentle burbling of a small stream that runs through it. As beautiful as it is, it's huge and confusing. I drove around for a while, and tears began to flow down my cheeks. I just wanted to visit my sweet grandson, and it hurt my heart so deeply that I couldn't find his grave. As a last resort, I called Isaac's mama and asked if she could direct me. She sent a few screenshots of the cemetery layout, but it was still unclear to me, and so I Facetimed her so she was able to walk me along the exact route to get to where his resting place is. When I arrived, I arranged the toy tractors and cows I'd brought him and sat next to his gravestone. I talked to him, cried over him, and sang him "Farmer in the Dell" and "Old McDonald" at the top of my lungs. Finally being able to sing to him and to bring him a few gifts was uniquely healing.

Some of my children and I have relationships that have become strained and as a result, I'm not involved in their lives or in the lives of their children. It grieves me deeply, but although I may not see some of my grandchildren, as their Nona I still pray that someday things will change, and I will be able to be a part of their lives. They carry some of my DNA, so I know in my heart I am with them always.

My son's kids are the ones who run to me and ask for gum. It's the first thing out of their mouths, but right after they always hug me and tell me I am pretty. I don't demand that my grandchildren hug me or kiss me because I already know they love me. I want them to feel safe with me. A few of my grandchildren have journals I've given them so that every time I'm at their house, I can sit and write a letter to them, and once they're older they'll have a whole collection of letters from Nona to read and cherish. I love reading to my grandchildren; it's one of my favorite things. I think reading expands their little minds, and it allows me to share special time with them. I've traveled with some of them, and we've had the adventures of a lifetime. There is something special about the one-on-one time together, from the cute conversations we share to the cherished

moments that are just between us. I've been able
to share my faith with my grandchildren who are
old enough to understand. I run around their
homes singing Sunday school songs that I've
learned from my own Sunday school days. One of
my sons once told me that he was singing the B-I-
B-L-E and one of my grandkids ran up to him and
solemnly said, "You can't sing that. That is
Nona's song." I once was telling one of my
grandsons how Jesus washes our dirty hearts, and
he woke up in the middle of the night, asking me
if Jesus would wash his heart again since he ate
chocolate. I've seen some of the prettiest parts of
the United States with my grandchildren. My
oldest grandson and I visited Mt. Rushmore
together and drove amongst the free-rein buffalo
in South Dakota. I swam with the dolphins with
another grandson and stayed in a teepee with two
of my other grandchildren. One of the coolest
things I was able to do was take two of my
grandchildren horseback riding for the first time at
the same place I took their daddy. That was a
special moment. Because I traveled so much for
work, my grandchildren thought I lived in hotels,
and whenever they could, they'd take advantage of
the hotel swimming pools and we'd spend hours
jumping on the beds.

I've been part of the tooth fairy association,
making up letters from where I live and telling my
grandchildren who lose a tooth that I called the
tooth fairy in my state and asked if they could

send the tooth fairy over state lines to give my grandchildren money since I'm not there. I've dressed up as the Grinch for my grandson's birthday party and walked around the neighborhood for him in the Grinch outfit. I once wore a dinosaur costume for another grandson's birthday and walked down the street in it, sweating and overheating, and knocked on his door. I've even dressed up as a Storm Trooper from Star Wars. I've purchased a cabbage patch doll for each one of my grandchildren and since they won't name any of their children after me, I made sure that either the first name or middle name was Bambi. I fixed them. When I purchased the Cabbage Patch Original at the hospital, the nurses couldn't stop laughing.

I have a grandson who loves Christmas and believes in Santa. My daughter wanted him to have one more year believing in Santa, so we took a trip to Colorado Springs to the vacation home of Santa Claus so he could meet him and believe Santa was real for one more year. My grandson was so overjoyed that he now knew where Santa spent his summers. I started a scrapbook with one of my granddaughters and when I visit, we scrapbook our pictures together so that in the future, she'll have something special that documents our times together.

I have a running joke with one of my grandsons where I call him stud muffin and in return, he'll call me blueberry muffin and it keeps on going. I

know I don't have many more years with my
oldest grandson since he'll be grown before long,
so every time I see him, I knock him to the ground
and wrestle him. We laugh so hard that sometimes
I have to run to the bathroom. It brings me so
much joy that he still tolerates his Nona's
shenanigans. I run around the house taking videos
of my grandchildren's stunts, and snapping their
pictures whenever they ask.

When my thirteenth grandchild was born, I was
with my daughter-in-love for the majority of it.
Although she ended up delivering at a hospital, I
spent hours and hours with her as she labored at
home, supporting her, encouraging her, and
holding her as she cried out in pain. Although she
may not be my biological daughter, going through
that experience with her, and caring for and
empathizing with her has created such an intimate
bond, and strengthened our overall relationship.

Whenever my children are going through
something, my heart hurts for my grandchildren.
You don't realize how much protection you have
over your grandchildren. I think that's why
grandparents soften the heartache of life. We're a
soft landing of sorts. It's not our job to train them,
but rather to pick up the extra load of prayer and
seek God on their behalf. They are the best
versions of us, and we want to protect that
precious cargo. It's funny with grandchildren; your
heart keeps growing bigger and bigger with each
one you have, and being a Nona never gets old.

For some reason, it seems to keep you young. That is, until you return to your own home and crash from the exhaustion you were too busy to notice.

They are my bundles of joy, sass, and have more energy than I could ever hope to, but the tenderness of their hearts continues to melt mine. I know why God gives us grandchildren. It's our second chance to live again and to correct the mistakes we made as parents through those little humans we call our grandkids. They are the fruit of our hard work as parents. We planted the seed in our own children, and now get to reap the blessings.

Grandchildren are truly the blessing we look forward to most in our older years. If my children want to keep them coming, I have enough space in my heart for expansion. They can take over my whole heart if they wish because I am their Nona, and they can have whatever they want.

The Map

Not long before my sons left for the military, I started traveling a little bit, first for the Census Bureau and then for the company I work for now. Occasionally I was able to take the twins with me, and after I was done with whatever work I had to do, we'd go sightseeing.

Some of my fondest memories are traveling with my sons, and even traveling alone. When I looked in the pocket of my heart and saw a map of the United States, I knew that that gift was placed there because it turned out to be the thing that got me through the loneliness of adjusting to an empty nest. It helped me discover myself and gave me a foothold in my life.

As I write this, I've been to 42 states and plan to visit the remaining eight states before I travel abroad. As Americans, we've been blessed with a truly beautiful country; places that take your breath away, places that can only be appreciated if you're physically standing there looking at it, and places that no camera could ever do justice.

After being with my children for the past two decades, I found myself living my life afraid and unsure. I was scared to be alone, but I knew that staying in the confines of my home or in the four walls of my hotel room would never help me. I began to look for out-of-the-box things to do to help me conquer my fears and to truly thrive, rather than just live. I vividly remember seeing a statement somewhere that read, "Leave no doubt." I took it as "Why not go skydiving?" *Why not? Why not jump out of a plane at 13,000 feet? Doesn't everyone do that?* Not long after, I took one of my daughters to an award ceremony with one condition: she had to go skydiving with me. Jumping out of that plane at 13,000 feet in the air while trusting the parachute to open and hoping that the instructor I jumped with had everything under control is something I will never do again. I can definitely put it on my resume as one of the stupidest things I've ever done, but also one of the bravest. I'm not sure if my daughter will ever forgive me for making her endure that stunt.

Wherever I'd go for work, I'd look up things to do around the area during my time off. I have seen breathtaking waterfalls while hiking in the mountains and I have basked in the icy cold waters beneath them, and left feeling more refreshed than I had in a long while. I've wandered off the beaten path on trails that led me to monuments of filing cabinets and other strange things that made me ask myself why someone would do it. I've been to Hollywood, strolled along the Walk of Fame, and pondered the people honored there and how they got a star for just living their best lives. I've been to wine country in California where I was dared to do a mud bath at a spa, where you find yourself in the nude with people you don't even know and recline in a tub full of mud to relax as all you can think about is why you put yourself in that situation, only to finish the process and realize that it was pretty cool and you'd do it again. I've walked the Golden Gate Bridge thinking about all the individuals who have taken their lives and wondering what brought them to that point where they'd lost all hope. What was it that made them decide that life was too much, or that made them refuse to wait one more moment or one more day to have the pressure subside and the realization that life *is* worth living? I remember crying on that bridge because I have my own story of wanting the pain to end.

I've climbed the grandest mountains and looked down on majestic views, knowing there *is* a God. One mountain I hiked was at a military base where my son was stationed. As we reached the summit, we found several large boulders with John 3:16 spray painted on them, and a cross standing in the middle. As I looked at that memorial of sorts, I knew I was on holy ground and began to pray. It was there that, when I lost my grandson, my son went up and wrote his

name on those same rocks. It's the one mountain
I wish I had the opportunity to climb again.

I've visited the Alamo and was confused at
first, almost thinking it *couldn't* be in the right
place, as the city has grown up around it. I've
sailed to different islands; places that tell the
story of our country and of those before us who
fought for freedom. I've gone to the Statue of
Liberty and Ellis Island, imagining the lives our
ancestors lived before they made that journey
and touched the ground of freedom. I wondered
if they'd thought it was worth the sacrifice and if
they'd gotten what they came for. I went to the
Field of Dreams movie set and thought about my
own dreams and if I'd held back with any of
them because I was so scared of failure. I drove
to the Sequoia National Forest with my son and
his wife at the time and nearly ran out of gas in
the process. I had no idea that once we reached
the park it was still another 35 miles to where the
trees were. On my way back, I was grateful I
could coast downhill to the nearest gas station. I
couldn't believe how big those trees were, or
how protected they were. I wish other natural
landmarks had the protection those trees do. One
of the trees even had a road through it. They
were a sight to see and made me marvel in awe
of God's creation.

I traveled to Palm Springs, CA, and took a
tramway up the mountain. I wandered around up
there, with no phone service and a phone camera
that couldn't even come close to capturing the
majestic views. I went to find the statue of
Marilyn Monroe only to learn it had been moved

in order for the city to build a casino. I've been to Maine, where the lobster is to die for, and the unique beauty of the state is something you can never forget. I met a woman who collected umbrella cases from all over the country. She was so passionate about her collection and she even made it into the Guinness Book of World Records. When I got home, I wrote a story about one of my cases and sent it to her. If she had that much passion for her collection, I wanted to take part in it with her.

I've gone to Philadelphia and walked the streets of our forefathers, wondering if they were able to sleep at night with all the pressure of writing the Constitution and ensuring a future of liberty and justice for their country. I took a carriage ride through the city and saw the houses of famous patriots, and wondered if I'd been there if I would've been one of them. Could I have been part of the revolution, standing up for freedom? Would I have made a difference and been willing to count the cost of making that difference? I've climbed lighthouses, looked out over the water, and realized just how much the title of *Lighthouse Keeper* entails, the sacrifices they made for the safety of the lives aboard the ships that passed, and the loneliness they must've endured for the sake of others' wellbeing.

One of the prettiest cities I've been to is St. Augustine: the oldest city in the United States. I took a carriage ride there and learned the history of it; the wars, slavery, suffrage, and the tension between the Catholics and the Protestants that resulted in the Protestants being prohibited from burying their dead within the walls of the fort. I walked the streets that haven't changed all that much since the days of the revolution when they were owned by Spain. I drank water from the Fountain of Youth but didn't feel any younger. Perhaps sulfur had a different effect on me than it did on others. I visited one of the oldest jails and experienced how they had to live in small quarters with no fresh air to breathe. The city is beautiful at Christmas. The magic of the season is almost tangible in the air as you travel through the city. I saw the largest thermometer in the world in Baker, CA while on my way to the Grand Canyon. I met someone that was from the same area I grew up in and we've stayed Facebook friends. I continued on to the canyon with my son and his wife at the time. When we arrived, the view took my breath away. I'd dressed for pictures and not warmth like I always do, and it was *so* cold that day, but I couldn't stop staring at the splendor of those mountains. There were no guardrails on the rocks at the edge of the canyon and I was shaking and so scared when I climbed onto a rock for a picture. I can still close my eyes and see those mountains. I would've loved to capture just the right shot to show others what I saw but only your eyes can hold those memories, and pictures just give you a glimpse of the awe that is found there. The Hoover Dam made me feel almost the same way, only it was manmade, and the canyon was formed by a word from God. The dam was overwhelming, thinking of the lack of tools and safety precautions they had back when it was built, and yet there were only a few losses during the construction. How did our country become what it is with so little technology?

I took trips to each of the Laura Ingalls family homesteads. I listened to their stories of how they built their homestead after the journey west in search of a better life, the tragedy and triumph they experienced along the way, and the joy they found as well as the heartache. I've seen buffalo in their natural habitat and drove through the middle of a herd of them in South and North Dakota. I saw Mount Rushmore with my oldest grandson and drove through a mountain that was called the Eye of the Needle. I visited the Devil's Tower in the state of Wyoming, where my grandson and I walked the two-and-a-half miles around it in sandals and crocs. We had no idea what we were doing when we started driving that morning. I saw the biggest milking cow and buffalo sculptures in North Dakota and drove the enchanted highway where a man had built sculptures along it because they needed something in North Dakota for people to go. I took one of my grandsons through Kansas, following the yellow brick road to prove there is no place like home. We drove to Colorado Springs and saw Pikes Peak twice together, once by train and the other by jeep. We had a magical time, and the sights from the very top of the mountain were something to behold if you could handle the low oxygen levels. I took my grandson to the Garden of the Gods where we played among the beauty of the rocks. I've said many times how the beauty of our country has taken my breath away and this place was no different. My grandson wasn't scared at all to climb the rocks and explore them. It was a once-in-a-lifetime chance after all. We drank water from the springs and felt refreshed by the stunning landscape and fresh mountain air. My grandson and I drove past Tupelo, Mississippi: the birthplace of Elvis Presley. We hadn't showered in 36 hours, but I knew we had to turn around and go visit Elvis' home. I've always had an enduring love for Elvis because he and I share the same birthday.

I spent time in Wisconsin where I went to a cheese castle where the most incredible cheese cuds were made. I drove through Iowa and stopped at the World's Largest Truck Stop. I've walked the streets of Washington D.C. and marveled at the awe-inspiring architecture. I've visited all three space centers, but the one in Huntsville, Alabama is the one I enjoyed the most. I was able to take boat rides on both the Mississippi and Missouri rivers and gone boating through the swamps.

My daughter-in-love and I took a trip to Casey, Illinois where the World's Largest Mailbox has earned its place in the Guinness Book of World Records. Every year, they add one large item to draw in the tourists. I've visited man-made cities and attractions such as Disneyland, Disney World, Sea World, the Vegas Strip, downtown Chicago, New York City, Los Angeles, and many more, but nothing compares to the beauty of creation that I hold in my heart. I've taken helicopter rides, boat rides, train rides, and hot air balloon rides all across our beautiful country, and I began taking horse-drawn carriage rides in every city I could.

Creation speaks to us in a way that man-made things cannot. Taking in the moment as you stand at the top of a mountain, the peace that floods over you as you stand at the edge of the ocean when there is just you and that great expanse of water, majestic mountains with the sun setting behind them, painting the sky all shades of fiery oranges and reds; these are where answers are found. They are where I've found bravery, I've found peace, and where the long, hard climbs and the roar of waterfalls brought me to a place of solitude when I was distraught.

My journeys have redefined me. They molded and fashioned a part of me that was missing. They left me feeling complete in some way like I'd shown up for *me*. I learned lessons along the way. I learned that I was courageous, that I held the courage to let go of beliefs I had just because it was common and to ask questions and search out my own answers—my own truth. I learned to live life with bravery. I got into a car with my GPS and just drove. I slept at rest stops with no fear of something happening to me. I met people along the way that changed me, and I hope I changed them. I had to start living outside my box and train myself to get up and go out. I had to change my thought process and believe there was something out there for me. I had to go out and not feel sorry for myself and learn to accept my new identity where my purpose was no longer a mom, teacher, wife, friend, or any other labels I carried. I had to embrace *Bambi* and find out who she was outside of all that. It's a process I'm still learning but getting better at.

The treasure of that map was my adventure of a lifetime. It was my God saying, "I have something more for you." He gave me the direction I needed to find myself and to experience myself in my own skin. I have a lot more to learn and I know God has many more places to take me. My life is an adventure of its own, and God is my GPS. The gift of the map in my pocket was an adventure for me to have at every corner. A treasure from Him alone.

The Round Table

When I first saw the round table, I didn't understand what it was for or how it would affect my life in the years to come. Years passed, and eventually, I came to understand exactly *why* that table was amongst the treasures in my heart. That table, so seemingly insignificant, was where I grew. It's where I learned countless life lessons, and where I found compassion and gave it in return. It was at that table that life stories were poured out and healing began. That round table was shared with strangers who, although we'd never met before, became part of me when I sat around their tables with them.

For the last fifteen-plus years, I have been in hundreds if not thousands of homes for work, first with the Census Bureau and then with Nielsen, the

data company. I have knocked on all kinds of
doors, been in all kinds of homes, and seen things
that people wouldn't believe if I told them. I have
experienced emotions I didn't even know I had and
have been changed from the inside out for the
better. These tables have shaped me, molded me,
and helped me to grow into a version of me I didn't
even know was possible. These tables have
become a part of me.

I have sat at tables for work, but it became
something so much deeper than just a job. It
became my purpose and my innermost desire to
bring hope to people that others have cast aside
and discarded as if they were nothing more than a
worn-out pair of socks, and not just that, but it
allowed me to bring my brokenness to the
forefront of my heart. Their stories and life
experiences helped *me* to pick up my own broken
pieces and heal.

I coined the phrase, "Changing lives one door
at a time," but these homes and their stories
actually changed mine. The stories of raw
humanity tug at your heart, and you can't walk
away from them and *not* feel changed. These
individuals, each with a past and a story, let their
emotional dam break, sometimes to the point
they would collapse in my arms, sobbing like a
child in the arms of their mother.

*A stranger becomes a friend as we pour our
stories out. The connection of two souls
searching for a sense of respect; for significance.*

Perhaps it's easier to spill our hearts to a stranger, because after all, what do we have to lose? We probably won't see each other again, but for a moment in time we are connected and forever changed in the releasing of our stories of pain, sadness, and victory. Not all stories are sad: some are of joy unspeakable, they are raw connections, and a way to share our hearts. People just want to be heard. They want to be assured that they matter, and a stranger knocking on their door can do just that. I can give them a voice and a platform when I sit down at their table, and say, "Tell me your story," or when I walk around their home and ask about the pictures on their walls. We all want to talk about ourselves but often bottle things up because we feel like we're bothering people, or perhaps they just don't care to listen. The gift I had and still have in going to peoples' homes allows me to knock on doors, ready to be their audience as they pour out their hearts. I have met so many people with years of marriage under their belt and asked them how they did it. I listened to their stories: some gave funny answers, some shared their hearts, and others, while looking deeply into their partner's eyes, simply stated, "That's what you do," and I could see the almost tangible love that had kept them going through thick and thin. I've been in homes and heard the phone ring and saw the utter devastation in the eyes of the one who answered the call. The cancer was back. I stood there, ready to listen, to cry with them, to whisper gently, "Let yourself grieve," and if needed, to give them space and time to come to terms with the news. I've held the hands of people grieving the recent loss of a spouse or a child and shared in their pain, our tears mingling as they searched for a way to begin living life again. I knocked on the door of a woman who had just moved into the house with her children after fleeing **her abuser** on a Greyhound bus. She told me they'd run away with only the clothes on their backs from her spouse who threw her down the stairs, and she had said enough. She had two daughters, one of whom was blind. I sat on the ground in her front yard and listened to the bravest and most courageous woman I'd ever met. We shared stories and locked arms with each other, knowing we were brave and had a story to tell the world: we had *survived*. I met a woman who had lived in Australia and became homeless with her daughter. They'd lived in a tent, and she'd shower at a nearby gym before going job hunting. She had such a profound story and spoke life to me during a time when I was struggling just to get out of bed in the morning. After going to see her over and over, I almost gave up on her, but something told me to go back one more time. She was an angel to me, and I will never forget her.

Stories can be found everywhere, and my job continued to take me to them in the most unexpected places. I sat at the table of a woman who lived in public housing, and all it took was one question and the floodgates of her heart opened. She poured out her story of the heartache she'd experienced and the brokenness she couldn't seem to recover from. I listened to her as if both our lives depended on it, even as a roach fell from the ceiling and landed on the table in front of me. I cared more about her tears than I did that roach. I've knocked on doors and when they opened, all I could see was poverty. It was in the children who looked hungry and unkempt, the mothers who, despite their best efforts, were overwhelmed and exhausted, and in the general disarray of their homes. It was as if a tornado of life had ripped through, leaving havoc in its wake, and they'd never been able to pick up the pieces. All of them had a story, and I sat at their tables and listened. The emptiness in their eyes testified to the abuse and the pain they suffered. Their brokenness was swallowing them up; they yearned to be heard, but the world turned its back and looked away. These families *needed* to be seen, and God sent me to their doors just for that. I've been in enough homes now that I can sense the situation and when I need to listen, when I need to hold a hand, or when I need to hug the pain away. These are the people that have been rejected. The ones who

are laughed at and ridiculed behind their backs. They have stories that aren't pretty, and just when they needed a moment to catch their breath when life knocked them down yet again, I was sent to their door.My stories of the people I've encountered could go on forever. I once met the most amazing woman in Malibu. Up on a hill in a three-million-dollar home, she was living a life of rejection and shame. Her story broke my heart, and we sat on the floor and cried together as she continued her tale of suffering. As she curled up into a ball, utterly broken, the weight of it all was almost more than I could bear. Later on, I was shocked when I was given an invitation to her home.
She'd gotten my name off a letter from my company. I'll never forget her face as she thanked me for caring and for allowing her to be vulnerable. My job was to go into these homes and sign the families up for something, but for me, my 'job' took on something different every day. The stories and experiences I have from work are a whole book by themselves.

This treasure is different. It's special, yes, but it goes deeper than that. It's shaped me. It's taught me things I wouldn't have learned anywhere else. I've had to adjust some of my belief systems and reevaluate my preconceived ideas. It's helped me grow a thicker skin. Each experience has changed my heart in its own way. Every table I've sat at has taken a little piece of

me and given me one in return. They've
broadened my horizons and reshaped my
perspective on the true meaning of human
experiences. My heart has been touched and
changed in a million different ways. Just as a
touch of the hem of His garment can make us
whole, the hands I've held, the ones who needed
a break, the ones who just needed a listening
ear—they've shown me that's all it takes to
change a life. I'm forever changed by it all. I feel
like I've gotten a little glimpse of how God sees
all of us.

Take a chance. Listen to a story. Let your heart
open up to the world around you. The greatest
treasure *you* can give someone is a listening ear,
but be prepared: it's a gift that keeps on giving.

The Ocean

I could see the gentle waves and feel the stillness
of the water in the next pocket of my heart. I
reminisced, replaying in my head the times I
desperately ran to the water, asking God for
direction, and over and over, asking him *why*. I'd
sat at the beach with pen and paper, begging God to
speak to me. When life felt like it was swallowing
me up, I'd run to the peacefulness of the water,
trying to catch my breath. In the darkest part of the
night at the edge of the water, I sat with tears
streaming down my face. I asked God for a way to
escape. I wanted answers to my questions. I wanted
direction for my life. So many times, life led me to
the water, and if I didn't go I feel that life would've
led to my death. I often prayed to the Lord, assuring
him that it would be okay if I didn't wake up in the
morning. It would be okay if you could take this
pain away. Each time I'd pray those words, I would

awaken and feel drawn to the water. I'd walked along the beach, picking up sand glass, reminded that their smooth surfaces were once sharp and jagged. Someone had smashed the bottle, the water took it out to sea, and the waves moved over it over and over again until the sides were smooth and soft to the touch. What a true representation of our lives.

I was reminded that life is not easy. The waves spoke to my soul, coming in and going out, like each chapter of our lives. They led me to answers, and sometimes to the questions that I needed to ask. Water may go on forever, but there is always an island somewhere for rest; a place to recover from the crashing and breaking of life.

God has always shown up for me at the edge of the water, moving gently over my broken life, and bringing peace in those moments. I went to him when I got pregnant with my twins, and He showed up and showed me I was prepared for the double blessing. I didn't need to fear the process; He would lead me all the way. God showed up when I went to the water and screamed and yelled and cried until I didn't have any tears left to cry, devastated by my name and what it had cost me all these years. He displayed his great love in giving my name the meaning of 'Holy Child". He gave me purpose again. I ran to him when I was hit or choked or spit on by a man who was supposed to love me but instead took from me. I often ran to the water asking *why*. I ran with tears flowing down my face, looking for

answers. I ran to find direction and for God to
just take this life away from me. I struggled to
hear God in those days as I was told to just pray
more and keep seeking him and be silent and
win my husband without a word. How could I
do that when I was choked until I passed out, or
when I was spit on in my face because I
disgusted someone? I'd sat at the water for
hours believing that God had a way of escape.
I'd known my prayers would be answered at just
the right time. The water calmed me, helping
me to wait.

Every year I would find water on my birthday.
I needed to hear the voice of God for my coming
year ahead. I needed time to reflect on how far I
had come, to find out what the word for the year
ahead was. I asked him every year for the time
for me to write. When was my story going to be
put to words in the form of a book to be sold to
people who needed to hear my story to survive
theirs? I'd always walked away, disappointed that
it wasn't that year.

I knew there was a story inside of me and I
knew the time would come for it to be released
from my innermost, bringing peace to my soul.
The waves of the ocean reminded me that
nothing stays the same. The waves of life come
and go. The life we live has good waves that
calm you and other times the waves will be high,
warning you a storm is coming in. You can feel
it and see with your own eyes, knowing it's time
to prepare. Sometimes waves come in with a
rush, leaving you unprepared and forcing you to

pick up the pieces and rebuild. Other times, you sit by the waves feeling peace, and you can even float amongst them. People that love to surf the waves are always looking for *that* big one; the same one we want to run away from, fearing the pain it could bring. Perhaps, if we learned to ride them, we could see the waves differently; we could embrace them.

No one will escape the pain of a wave in their life. None of us will walk away without feeling the sharp edges of glass that need to be smoothed over. We'll all have a time that requires us to rebuild because of what the crashing of the waves has done in our lives. *But we will rebuild stronger and better.* I found my place by the ocean. I found a place for me to run to. I found the answers and heard the still small voice among the loudness of life. I found the place where I can come *just as I am* and He will carry me amongst the sand and lead me to stillness. I found my place where I go to rejoice; to sing of his goodness. The water is where life stands still, where it's held in place for a moment, enough for me to take a deep breath and walk again. This treasure that was hidden within a pocket of my heart is what has kept me going all these years because it speaks to my being, and it is there I am led to restore my soul.

Conclusion

Looking back at the span of my life, the hand of God is visible throughout all of it. When I thought I'd been forgotten, He reminded me He was always there. When I felt unloved, He showed me His love everlasting. When I thought I'd been abandoned, He never left my side, even when I couldn't see it.

These treasures He's given me have been my reprieve in the darkest times of my life. They were the air in my lungs when I couldn't breathe, gifts given to me to help me through a lifetime of sorrow and pain, and the things I needed to give me a glimpse into my Father's heart and see just how big it is. All of them were given to me at just the right moment.

When I look back over my life, I now find peace, realizing that none of it happened by chance. Every trial, every experience, and every struggle held a purpose. The journey of life is hard. We're not promised a life of rainbows and unicorns, but we are given things to help us when the going gets rough. It's not a

one size fits all situation, but rather a unique
and personal thing, with our gifts handpicked
by God, especially for us. Some of your
treasures would never have helped me get
through my life, and some of mine couldn't
help you. Our treasures are specially designed
just for us by our heavenly Father.

I am captivated by God's design for me and all
the treasures he placed inside my heart.
Each one had a part in teaching me to breathe,
to take a moment to relax, and to trust His
plan. There will always be storms, but we'll
come out on the other side, stronger for it. It'll
be dark, but the sun will always rise again.
Each one of my pocket-gifts perfectly
represents that: a beacon of hope shining
through the dark when the storm was so fierce
that I'd given up. I think all of this has
awakened a new perspective of God's love. He
is a loving God, and though He allows people
to make choices that lead to pain and suffering,
He will always provide a way of escape.

Treasures are hidden away, but when the
time is right you find them and rejoice in the
gift you found. My life was hard. I went
through things that no child should have to
endure. I experienced pain so brutal I didn't
know if I would survive it. I lost hope to the
point I didn't want to wake up the next morning.
Despite all this, as I look back on these
treasures, I can see the unconditional love that I
was given and it leaves no doubt in my mind: *I
was never alone.* My hope, as I bring this to a
close, is that these stories have helped you to

look for your own treasures. To not just see the brokenness in your life, but to see the hand of God *always* working on your behalf. I want this to bring you hope. I want you to learn, as I did, to look beyond the situation and see the blessing that came out of it. As cliché as this may sound, I want you to see the cup half full and not half empty. When you look at a seed, visualize the orchard it can bring forth. When you see a bunch of puzzle pieces, I hope you can now see the puzzle all put together the way it was meant to be. When you see lemons, instead of focusing on the sourness, imagine the sweetest lemonade. See what you can discover in the tragedies of life. See where your discoveries lead you. Allow the healing to happen and see things through a new lens. God has hidden your treasures in places you may not be able to see until He leads you to and unearths them.

I have so much life left to live; so many experiences left to have. I know at just the right moment God will show up with another treasure that He has hidden in my heart for such a time as this. I won't stop looking for them because I know they're all around me, but are just hidden right now. The treasures of my heart have led me to wholeness, and I hope yours do the same. Don't take them for granted: they will teach you to survive and thrive through this life. Cherish them—they're worth more than you can imagine, and all the little things in life you so often miss? You'll realize those are the true treasures in your heart. They always have been.

Thank you, dear reader, for becoming a part of my story by reading this! Your support and encouragement mean the absolute world to me. As a child, I never dreamed this day would come and yet here we are. Thank you for sticking with me up until this point! As we near the end of our time together, hold tight to this verse, Jeremiah 29:11:

**" For I know the plans I have for you, declares the LORD,
plans to prosper you and not to harm you, plans to give you hope, and a future."**

I am living proof that He really can give you hope and a future, regardless of how lost and desperate you may feel at this moment. From my heart to yours: thank you for joining me in my story. Don't ever be afraid to share yours!
Scan the QR code below and it will take you to an additional chapter-The Final Chapter-that is strictly available on my website. I hope to see you there, my friend!

The Final Chapter

Resources

Email: Josephine.ourstory@gmail.com
Website: HealingThroughStories.com
Facebook: The Journey of Josephine
Author's Personal Facebook: Bambi Lynn
Instagram: Lynn.Bambi
Domestic Violence Hotline: 800-799-7233
Suicide and Crisis Hotline: 988

As an author, the greatest gift I can ever receive is a simple review. If it is in your heart to leave a review via Amazon.com or one of my social platforms, I will be forever grateful!
And once again, I cannot thank you enough for joining me here. Without you, my readers, none of this would be possible!